Welcome to the EVERYTHING

These handy, accessible books give you all you need to tackle a difficult project, gain a new hobby, comprehend a fascinating topic, prepare for an exam, or even brush up on something you learned back in school but have since forgotten.

You can read an *EVERYTHING*® book from cover-to-cover or just pick out the information you want from our four useful boxes: e-facts, e-ssentials, e-alerts, and e-questions. We literally give you everything you need to know on the subject, but throw in a lot of fun stuff along the way, too.

We now have well over 100 *EVERYTHING*® books in print, spanning such wide-ranging topics as weddings, pregnancy, wine, learning guitar, one-pot cooking, managing people, and so much more. When you're done reading them all, you can finally say you know *EVERYTHING*®!

FACTS
Important sound bytes of information

SSENTIALS
Quick handy tips

ALERT
Urgent warnings

QUESTIONS?
Solutions to common problems

THE
EVERYTHING®
Series

Dear Reader,

It is with great pleasure that I bring you *The Everything® Scrapbooking Book*. I hope you enjoy reading it as much as I enjoyed writing it. Through this process I have met so many new and interesting people, all of whom agree that scrapbooking has helped them both to save family keepsakes and to make new acquaintances at the same time. We have chatted about the friendships that have blossomed through scrapbooking clubs, the fun that comes with creating new ways to show off family history, and the fulfillment that is a result of journaling daily experiences.

   I hope that this book allows you to encounter the same benefits of scrapbooking by providing you with a few ideas to jump-start your creative thinking process. It is designed to act as an introduction for the scrapbooking novice as well as a guide for experienced scrappers. My objective is to give you a valuable resource that you will turn to each time you want to try something new. Thank you for choosing this book to guide you along the way, and best of luck in your new adventure!

Happy scrappin'!

Jennifer Barr

THE
EVERYTHING®
SCRAPBOOKING BOOK

Creative ideas for preserving
memories that last a lifetime

Jennifer Barr

Adams Media Corporation
Avon, Massachusetts

EDITORIAL
Publishing Director: Gary M. Krebs
Managing Editor: Kate McBride
Copy Chief: Laura MacLaughlin
Acquisitions Editor: Bethany Brown
Development Editors: Lesley Bolton,
        Michael Paydos

PRODUCTION
Production Director: Susan Beale
Production Manager: Michelle Roy Kelly
Series Designer: Daria Perreault
Cover Design: Paul Beatrice and Frank Rivera
Layout and Graphics: Brooke Camfield,
    Colleen Cunningham, Rachael Eiben
    Michelle Roy Kelly, Daria Perreault

An Everything® Series Book.
Everything® is a registered trademark of Adams Media Corporation.

Published by Adams Media Corporation
57 Littlefield Street, Avon, MA 02322 U.S.A.
www.adamsmedia.com

ISBN: 1-58062-729-3
Printed in the United States of America.

J   I   H   G   F   E   D   C   B   A

Library of Congress Cataloging-in-Publication Data
Barr, Jennifer.
The everything scrapbooking book : creative ideas for preserving
memories that last a lifetime / Jennifer Barr.
p.   cm.
ISBN 1-58062-729-3
1. Photograph albums. 2. Photographs—
Conservation and restoration. 3. Scrapbooks. I. Title.
TR465 .B37   2002
745.593—dc21   2002008443

Many of the designations used by manufacturers and sellers to distinguish their products are claimed as trademarks. Where those designations appear in this book and Adams Media was aware of a trademark claim, the designations have been printed in initial capital letters.

This publication is designed to provide accurate and authoritative information with regard to the subject matter covered. It is sold with the understanding that the publisher is not engaged in rendering legal, accounting, or other professional advice. If legal advice or other expert assistance is required, the services of a competent professional person should be sought.
—From a *Declaration of Principles* jointly adopted by a Committee of the
American Bar Association and a Committee of Publishers and Associations

Illustrations by Barry Littmann.

This book is available at quantity discounts for bulk purchases.
For information, call 1-800-872-5627.

Visit the entire Everything® series at everything.com

Contents

Dedication

To my loving and supportive husband, daughter, family, and friends.

Acknowledgments

Many thanks to everyone who helped make this book possible by donating their artwork, time, and ideas, especially Tom Barr, Lucille DeFrancesco, Michele Niec, Patricia and William Barr, Beth and Bill Barr, Amanda Barr, Matthew Barr, Jessica Faust, Jennifer Reid, R. Eric Jarrell, Michele and Greg Poruban, Mellisa Stanislaw, Dr. Ann Oland, Andrea Gintert, All About Scrapbooking in Downingtown, Pennsylvania, Fiskars, Inc.

Introduction

From basic storage theories to difficult scrapbooking techniques, preserving your memories and family heritage can be both rewarding and fun. Chances are you have a memory box somewhere in your attic full of old concert tickets, photos from college, or Broadway play programs. Most of the materials that you have collected have probably been long forgotten as they sit quickly deteriorating in a damp or otherwise unhealthy environment. This is your opportunity to learn about the best ways to take your old memories and transform them into something personal and expressive that you can share with friends and family. You will find that as you complete each scrapbook page, you will want to immediately show your artwork to loved ones. You will enthusiastically leave your albums on the coffee table for guests to flip through.

The most enjoyable part of your decision to begin scrapbooking is the opportunity it gives you to travel down memory lane as you sift through and organize old photographs and memorabilia. While you are having fun, you will also be learning about the most important aspects of scrapbooking by safely preserving past and future memories.

The Everything® Scrapbooking Book will teach you basic techniques about the three major elements of modern scrapbooking: safety, journaling, and imagination. Beyond these basic guidelines, however, there are no boundaries to either the craft of scrapbooking or your imagination. This book will help you to create your own style of preserving family heritage.

Modern scrapbooking is now over a decade old, but no one can claim to have discovered this popular craft. While the word scrapbooking has just recently started to be used as a verb, the idea of scrapbooks dates back thousands of years. It has been documented as a favorite pastime of writers, presidents, and other famous individuals throughout history. You have probably developed some sort of scrapbook album over the years, and chances are you did not need anyone to show you the way. This book is designed to teach you the importance of archival quality materials, the design of basic tools, the details of creative techniques, and the elements that make your scrapbook individual. The rest is up to you!

This is also a wonderful craft to begin in conjunction with learning about your family history and documenting your genealogy. These factual elements, coupled with a creative aspect, provide the key that keeps people interested and coming back for more. Every layout page is different, and each album has its own personality. Once you get hooked on scrapbooking, you will probably find that it is something you never want to end.

Creative elements aside, this book will help you to find new pockets of scrapbooking and make new friends through the craft. It is a wonderful way to meet new people, locate others who have the same interests, and discover lifelong friends. You will find that you look forward to attending all-night crops, and before long you might even consider going on a scrapbooking getaway weekend. It is truly a craft that brings people together.

Overall, *The Everything® Scrapbooking Book* will help guide your way through the craft with detailed descriptions of tools, techniques, and money-saving tips. Use it for inspiration, and keep it at your scrapbooking workstation for a quick and easy reference!

CHAPTER 1

Laying the Foundation

Whenever we begin a new project or adventure, we instinctively look at the history of the activity in order to get answers to some basic questions. It is only natural to search for the foundation of our ideas. What force drove you to start this project? Why does it interest you? And what can you get out of it?

Defining a Trend

Scrapbooking is the act of creating valuable and memorable keepsake albums that will safely preserve some of your most intimate and important memories. These albums not only contain photographs of memorable events, they also help you tell the whole story through journaling and souvenirs. Modern scrapbooking is a billion-dollar industry that encompasses hundreds of elements and options. However, behind all of the company literature and Internet sites, today's scrapbooking boils down to three primary concepts:

- Protection
- Imagination
- Journaling

Safety and Scrapbooking

If you look back at memory books from your grandparents, parents, or even from high school or college, you will undoubtedly see yellowed photographs, fragile newspaper clippings, and brittle adhesives. Most of these are caused by a reaction to paper with acid. Modern scrapbooking focuses on archival quality materials. This terms refers to materials that contain no acid, are pH balanced, and that contain no solvents.

Throughout this book you will find safety details about items as they are described. In the meantime, we can start with a few things to help you understand the importance of putting safety first.

Lignin is a material found in trees that holds together wood cells. If not removed from paper processing, it will cause the document to brown, crumble, and eventually to break down completely.

Acid is the most harmful culprit in scrapbooking. It will not only damage one part of a scrapbook page, it will migrate to another. Papers and materials must all be acid-free and buffered for stability.

The adhesives used in magnetic albums contain acids that will destroy photographs. These acids also tend to move to other areas of your album and cause destruction. Non-permanent adhesives are sometimes mistakenly used in scrapbooks. They are not recommended either because of their unstable and temporary nature. Using rubber cement and similar adhesives will ultimately prove frustrating, since once you finish a scrapbook you will have to go back and administer a different adhesive.

Unless a pen is labeled as being safe or acid free, chances are good that it contains corrosive material or other solvents that will be damaging to the paper and photos. That damage will spread to other areas of your scrapbook. Ballpoint and felt-tip pens that do not say acid-free are not safe. Similarly, inks that contain water can be hazardous and could cause running or smearing.

Journaling

Photo of journaling style.

Photo of alternate journaling style.

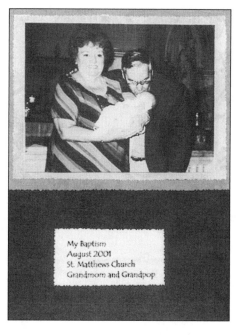

Journaling is a great way to tell a story, record its details, and truly preserve the memory. It may become something more interesting for future generations to cherish or something you yourself giggle over in ten years. Unless you want to, writing the story does not mean that you have to describe it in diary fashion. It simply means recording something more than what the picture or souvenir possesses. For example, here are two ways to describe this photo. Neither one is right or wrong, but you will notice a clear difference in style. Regardless of how you decide to journal, the technique preserves much more of the memory than simply presenting the picture.

Let the Imagination Run Wild

One of the biggest mistakes that new scrappers make is not allowing themselves the opportunity to be creative with their materials. Scrapbooking is a big business. If you become inundated with company literature, mailings, or other outside influences, it is easy to get out of touch with your own unique sense of style and personality. Don't get me wrong: outlets that provide us with the tools of scrapbooking are a necessity, but it is important to have a little confidence in yourself before using a template or copying an idea. Save these resources for when you are really stuck.

ESSENTIALS

Newspapers are made from a low-quality paper and will be one of the first items to decompose in a scrapbook. To preserve newspaper clippings, use a de-acidification spray that will remove the acid. To be on the safe side, make a backup photocopy of the article on off-white paper for a traditional look.

Why Scrapbooking?

Why have you decided to start scrapbooking, or, if you haven't decided, why should you start? There are many reasons to start this hobby, but the only person who knows what's most important is you. Many people begin by stumbling onto the trend accidentally. They start to organize their photographs and find themselves in a craft store sifting through hundreds of styles of albums. One thing leads to another and all of a sudden they have started a new hobby. What began as a simple need for organization often flourishes into a desire to tell a story and safely preserve their memories for future generations.

Here lies the basis for our need and the answer to our question "why": history and future generations. We all want to keep memories alive, remember the good times, and reflect on our lives. Sometimes we even feel that if we throw out a concert ticket or a Broadway play program, we will then forget we attended the event at all. Scrapbooks help us to preserve our most cherished memories for ourselves and for years to come.

As albums are refurbished, many use a pH testing pen to analyze the level of acidity in their materials. While this is an important step, pH testing pens work by turning a color to show the level of acidity and can leave marks on the scrapbook. Since some of your pieces may be heritage pieces and are almost guaranteed acidic, skip this step and make the assumption that the materials need to be buffered.

Like it or not, one day we won't be around anymore to tell our story, whether it's the history of the family, how you met your spouse, or any other significant event of your life. Sure, a story might get passed down through generations, but will the details? For example, you might know that your ancestor was a general in the Civil War. Wouldn't it be wonderful to know some details about his life, how he fared in the war, or some stories of combat or history that we can otherwise only read in textbooks? If he had kept a journal or scrapbook, would it not be a treasure in your family? Anyone can know the headlines, but what happens to the story? This is where modern scrapbooking shines. We have come to understand the importance of detail and know the significance of telling a story.

An Added Bonus

Once we understand the meaningfulness of scrapbooking, it is wonderful to find all of the other countless advantages that come from the pastime! "Scrappers," a term that is generally used to describe those who devote a significant amount of time to scrapbooking, often find themselves surrounded by people who share a love for the craft. Many feel that scrapbooking provides a valuable service to the family while also being fun and creative. It is always a treat to find someone else who has the same passion for the subject.

Hundreds of friendships have resulted from scrapbooking. People often share each other's company at crops, events that brings together scrappers of all types to communicate ideas and concepts. Formal scrapbooking clubs or company representatives will also hold crops to help promote their own materials or causes, but the events often feel less like marketing events than like gatherings of friends.

A History of Scrapbooks

While modern scrapbooking is a unique billion-dollar industry, its roots have a long and interesting history that can be dated back hundreds of years. If we look back far enough, we find that the word album dates to Greek and Roman times.

FACTS

Giorgio Vasari's *Lives of the Most Eminent Italian Architects, Painters, and Sculptors* is not only where many believe scrapbooking originated, but his ideas are sometimes considered the stepping-stone to modern libraries and museums.

According to a Tulane University study, the process we know as scrapbooking began in medieval times. Back then, scribes were known to create bound emblem books that included drawings and interpretations. It was in the 1500s that scrapbooking started to take a more modern look and shape. In his book *Lives of the Most Eminent Italian Architects, Painters, and Sculptors,* a man named Giorgio Vasari supported the idea that artists should keep and record their works in albums.

"Commonplace" Books

After the 1500s, we find a great deal of documentation on something called "commonplace" books. These were books that were first started as a place to record quotations, passages, and phrases. Writing around the year 1600, Shakespeare directs Hamlet to enter the words "Smile, and smile, and be a villain" in his commonplace book. According to Shakespeare, commonplace books were a place where "intellectual young men . . . recorded good sayings and notable observations."

FACTS

"Granger Books" were a hot trend that died quickly after hitting a peak of popularity. The trend began when William Granger published *The Biographical History of England* in 1769 and included prints that illustrated his text. In future editions, he added extra blank pages that the book owner could then personalize with illustrations, autographs, letters, or thoughts.

The trend was steady. In 1685, the famous poet and author John Locke wrote a letter to a friend about his technique of constructing and indexing a commonplace book. Originally written in Latin, it was translated and published in 1706 as *New Method of Making Common-Place Books in French, English, and Dutch.* The book described the best ways to maintain proverbs, ideas, references, mediations, speeches, quotations, and so on. This fueled the interest and popularity of these books. Commonplace books are widespread among historical figures, and finding these treasures often means we retrieve a great deal of the past. John Pendleton Kennedy had his commonplace books donated to the Peabody Institute and sealed until 1901. It is well documented that Thomas Jefferson enjoyed gathering newspaper clippings of his presidency and placing them in a leather-bound plain paper book. W. E. B. DuBois noted in his book *The Philadelphia Negro; A Social Study* that much of his research was indebted to William Dorsey and his creation of about 300 scrapbooks and commonplace books that provided a record of the lives of turn-of-the-century African-Americans.

Friendship Albums

Men were not the only influences on the modern scrapbook. Women began to take up the hobby in the early 1800s by pasting quotes and phrases when something called the "Friendship Album" became en vogue. These were commonly used as a place to keep well-wishes to and from friends, poetry, autographs, and even recipes. It was a popular feminine pastime, and women often kept locks of hair, letters, and cards from friends.

During a 1999 study of the history of women in Ireland, researchers found that much of the information they sought was obtainable only through commonplace books and friendship albums. They found that Irish women recorded their personal lives in these books, which included paintings, stitching, embroidery, plays, poems, music, and many other individual effects.

Scrapbooks

As new ways of printmaking were discovered, so were new techniques to save printed materials. The term scrapbook was coined in the Victorian era and was derived from brightly colored paper called scrap. These German-developed die-cut glossy products were developed through a process called chromolithography and could be purchased from specialty shops. Manufacturers used this paper to help sell products, and die-cuts that used popular images such as flowers, animals, and birds were sold directly to the public. Die-cuts were the catalyst to a scrapbooking phenomenon that can be compared to any popular fad today.

Scrapbooks were also known as ways of saving original documents in a personal collection. They sometimes acted as a filing cabinet for organizing bills and checks. They were also used to save other printed material that was deemed important, such as certificates of birth, marriage, graduation, and death. Calling cards, advertisements, tickets, calendars, and programs were also widely collected.

The 1880s were an important decade in the history of scrapbooks. Once newspapers and photography were invented and began gaining popularity, the common look of scrapbooks began to take shape. In 1880, when the Kodak camera became available, E. W. Gurley published a book called *Scrap-Books and How to Make Them.* In his book he notes that Americans now had 8,000 newspapers to read, and he comments on the foolishness of letting a good article go to waste. A serial called The Scrapbook was issued in 1885. It rendered the pastime as a hobby for preserving pictures and newspapers in a blank book.

FACTS

In 1872, Mark Twain, who some described as being too preoccupied with collecting quotes and articles about himself, patented "Mark Twain's Patent Scrapbook." By 1901, fifty-seven styles of his album were available. His books included self-pasting pages featuring gummed lines that could be dampened with a small amount of water.

In the early 1900s, publishers began to market scrapbooks to the masses, developing dedicated themes including school, college, motherhood, bridal, and First Communion. Some books were dedicated to fads such as postcards or collages, but the basic form of the scrapbook continued on its popular course, particularly with the growing popularity and continued ease of photography. Toward the middle of the century the trend started to turn to photograph albums, and little or no space was devoted anymore to the other souvenirs that had formerly been scrapbook staples.

The Current Collector

The trend of current scrapbooking is often cited as beginning when Creative Memories, a direct-sales company, began to market scrapbooks in 1987. While this is the major event that created scrapbooking in the modern sense of the word, the resurgence truly began in the 1970s with the renewal of interest in family history.

The science of tracing roots, called genealogy, was pioneered by the Mormon population and its reliance on scrapbooks. In scrapbooking terms, the science of genealogy came to fruition in 1980 during a conference in Salt Lake City, where many family scrapbooks were exhibited. This called for new products and safety methods for protecting documents and pictures. The magnetic photo albums and self-adhesive pages that had been so popular were discovered to be unsafe and to be destroying memories at a fast pace instead of preserving them.

ESSENTIALS

Archival Mist is a product that neutralizes the destructive acids in paper and deposits a safe, permanent alkaline buffer to protect against future acid attack.

The request for safe products caused a snowball effect for companies that had been supplying crafts for years. These organizations were now forced to catch up to the industry leaders and provide quality creative items for hungry scrapbookers.

Housewives with good ideas and business sense began starting companies, inventing tools, marketing their ideas, and selling scrapbooking materials. The industry looked for ways to endorse quality materials, and magazines popped up for the niche market. Within the decade, scrapbooking became known as one of the biggest moneymakers in the arts-and-crafts industry.

Today there are more than 400 privately owned scrapbooking stores across the country. Many offer classes and provide private instruction. Internet sites devoted to scrapbooking number in the hundreds, and clubs are popping up in every region of the country. Conferences and conventions are the newest events being planned for customers, clubs, retailers, company representatives, and friendships. Those who want to call scrapbooking a fad should probably take a closer look!

The ABCs of Scrapbooking

Throughout this book, and in any other place you spend time learning about scrapbooking, you will come across terminology that is specific to the craft itself. It is very important that you understand these concepts before really digging into the pastime. Below is a list of the common scrapbooking terms you will undoubtedly come across. Some other specific terms restricted to particular tools will be defined throughout this book.

Acid–Chemicals found in the fibers of papers that will cause the materials to become yellowed and easily broken. Acid has the ability to migrate to many parts of a scrapbook.

Acid-Free–Designation for materials that are effective in preserving memories from dangerous chemicals. These materials will contain alkaline material and have a pH level of 7 or higher.

Adhesive–A tool that must be acid-free, adhesives are used to hold layouts, pictures, die-cuts, and other scrapbooking materials in place.

Album–A blank book used as the main ingredient of scrapbooking.

Alkaline–The antonym of "acidic."

Archival–A term used by scrapbookers that describes whether a material is safe to use.

Buffered–Paper treated with calcium or magnesium carbonate, both alkaline agents that cause the product to be resistant to acid.

Calligraphy–A type of script that is cursive or angular.

Clip Art–Objects, designs, or artwork printed from a computer software program for use in layout pages.

Collage–Pasting on one page various materials not normally associated with one another.

Color Wheel–Colors of the spectrum arranged to show relationships with each other.

Crop–An event where many gather to work on scrapbooks together. These have often become times to socialize, share tools, reveal secrets, and simply make the process more fun.

Cropping–Trimming the edges of a photograph to fit into a layout, emphasize the subject, fit more pictures on one scrapbook page, or for artistic reasons.

Cut-Outs–Shapes that are meant to be cut out of a larger sheet of paper.

Cutting Mat—A surface placed onto a table on which you can safely cut paper and other materials.

De-acidification—A protective process that comes from chemical products created to neutralize acidic paper and add a buffer to make it archival quality.

Die-Cuts—Brightly colored material formed in shapes for use in layout pages.

Dye-Based Ink—Waterproof and pH-balanced ink that has a thin consistency and that creates a muted image when stamping.

Embossing—To decorate a surface with raised designs.

Emulsion—The coating on photographic film or printing paper. This is a light-sensitive material and is easily damaged by fingerprints, water, sun, or scratches.

Encapsulation—Placing treated paper or pictures between two sheets of polyester and fastening the sheets together to ensure a surrounding of archival-quality material.

Genealogy—A record of family ancestry.

Heirloom—A family possession passed on from generation to generation.

Heritage—Family traditions and history.

Journaling—The art of preserving memories through writing information about each memory in a scrapbook.

Kneaded Eraser—A soft eraser used to clean scrapbook pages of pencil after all work is completed.

Laminate—To overlay material with a thin clear plastic. Heat used in the lamination process can cause damage to pictures or souvenirs.

Lettering—Using your own writing on a scrapbook page, in basic journaling, or when creating captions and titles.

Lignin—A material found in plants that causes high levels of acidity in paper, it is often removed in the papermaking process. Newsprint and similar low-quality papers contain high levels of lignin.

Mount—Adhering a design and/or photo to a scrapbook page.

Paper Piecing—A pattern or figure made from many layers of paper cut into shapes.

Pedigree Chart—A diagram showing the lines of your direct ancestors.

Permanent Paper—Paper treated to resist corrosion from chemicals or acid.

pH Balanced—A measure of the levels of acidity or alkalinity in any scrapbooking material. Archival materials will contain a pH balance of 7 or higher.

Photographic Activity Test (PAT)—Predicts harmful interactions between scrapbooking products and photographic materials.

Photo-Safe—A term used by companies on packaging for scrapbooking materials or photo storage. Not considered as terminology that describes true archival material.

Pigment Ink—Rich, heavy ink that has a high archival quality and is often used for embossing.

Polyethylene—Clear plastic used in photo-preservation materials.

Polyester—Stable plastic used in photo preservation.

Polyvinyl Chloride (PVC)—A term synonymous with vinyl, a common plastic. Often used mistakenly in scrapbooks, this material emits destructive gases and causes harm. Safe products will contain a "PVC-free" label.

Pop-Ups—A three-dimensional object or design that rises when a scrapbook's page is opened.

Protective Sleeve—Plastic sleeves that protect scrapbook pages.

Punch-Art—Paper or other thin material cut with punches into shapes, combined into a pattern, and used to create a work of art for your scrapbook page.

PVC—See Polyvinyl Chloride.

Resin-Coated Paper—Specialized photographic paper containing plastic polyethylene that is used in many consumer film-processing plants due to its fast drying time. Resin-coated paper is not as ideal as fiber-based paper for developing prints.

Stamping—Using a rubber stamp and ink to decorate your scrapbook pages.

Stencil—A sheet of plastic or cardboard into which a desired lettering or design has been cut so the pattern can be recreated on the surface beneath.

Template—A pattern or mold serving as a guide for layouts.

Typography—The art of printing with type. Also means the appearance of printed matter.

Chapter 2
Affordable Scrapbooking

The biggest obstacle for beginners and longtime scrapbooking addicts alike is the cost. The price of necessities is sometimes high, and more often than not price becomes something that stands in the way of pursuing this hobby. Beginning this craft means learning when and where to splurge, why you can live without a few things, and how to save money and beat the system.

Starting with the Basics

There are truly only a few things you need to start scrapbooking. An album, paper (color and white), adhesive, scissors, and a pen are all that are really required to get you going. If you intend to splurge, do so with items you will use on a daily basis—the necessities that are the backbone of scrapbooking. Spending the extra money will help in the end, when quality can save you future headaches.

ESSENTIALS

Smart shopping includes buying in bulk. If you can find a SAM's CLUB, Costco, or BJ's near you, chances are that you will save money in some way. Some use these warehouses as a chance to get together with friends and split the cost of products, while others see it as an opportunity to store materials away until they are eventually needed.

Album costs can range from $12.95 to $65 or even higher depending on the size, style, brand, and extent of the fillers. For example, a 12" × 12" album from some specialty brands with the standard fifteen pages costs $36, but once you start adding page refills and protective sleeves, the album's price suddenly reaches heights you might not have originally considered.

Shop Around

Scrapbooking is a hobby that takes a great deal of time and not only on the creative end. The more time you spend shopping around for items at low or discount prices, the more you will save in the long run. Become familiar with companies or stores that offer discount racks, promotions, coupons, or special days on which to buy items at a rebate. Spend money carefully and without regrets. Remember, this is supposed to be fun and gratifying, and stress or guilt due to frivolous spending and shopping that was not well thoughtout can make this hobby seem more like a chore.

Local Scrapbooking Stores

Local scrapbooking stores and discount craft chains can really be lifesavers when it comes to saving on supplies. At Michaels arts and crafts store, they sell a 12" × 12" binder for $24.99 that is comparable to some of the specialty brands. Once you add refill packs and protective sleeves, you might find you've ventured into the $40 range, but you probably won't go any higher. This is a quality album, and while there are differences between this and others, it is a very good option if cost is an issue.

ESSENTIALS

Scrapbooking stores and craft-supply retail outlets will often honor each other's coupons. If you see a 40-percent-off coupon for a craft store outside your immediate area, clip it and try to use it at a store closer to home. Most chains will honor this request—you'll save the money and the mileage!

Important areas to stay away from in discount craft stores are products that do not have adequate information on the label. Looking for "Acid-Free" or "Archival Quality" is your number one priority. Some manufacturers skimp on the safety of their materials by allowing acid in their products, which they nonetheless advertise as scrapbooking materials. These are inferior, and you would be wise to spend your money on something more stable.

Direct Sales Companies

It is impossible to begin a hobby like scrapbooking without hearing about the direct sales companies associated with the craft. In fact, this is often where many people hear about it in the first place. This is big business, and while many companies cringe at the parallel, selling from "home shows" is really no different than throwing a Tupperware party. This is not a bad thing! Direct sales companies are a great place to start.

Most direct sales companies work by providing customers local consultants. If you contact the company directly, they will find a consultant in your area and refer you to him or her. Consultants have valuable information, and the products they provide are of very high quality. It is important, however, to keep in mind that their number-one goal is to sell you the company's product. While most have very good reputations and respect their customers, it is important to remember that they are in business. You should never be made to feel like you have to buy something.

It is easy to think of a scrapbooking company consultant as an expert on the subject, but this is not always the case. While consultants are well trained, they might not be experts in fields of photography, computer programs, genealogy, or other technical scrapbooking issues. Find a true expert to answer your specialized questions.

Home shows are a great place to get an introduction to scrapbooking. During these shows consultants often offer a basic scrapbooking workshop, giving a general but thorough idea of what the hobby entails. The rest of the time is for attendees to work on their books and socialize. Home shows are a great way to save some money too! If you offer to sponsor a show and provide a few friends, most consultants will give you a thank-you gift or a big discount on an item or two. Some consultants also provide door prizes. Who knows, you could be the lucky winner!

The Photo Fund

There are so many tools and materials to buy for scrapbooking that we often forget about the biggest long-term expense: developing photographs. Processing pictures costs money, and those of us on a budget usually forget about this expense in our eager anticipation of seeing the photos we recently dropped at a processing center.

The most expensive picture processing is at specialty photography stores. One twenty-four-exposure roll of 35mm film and double prints can cost up to $15.99. These photos are usually of the highest quality and standards, and often the stores that charge these prices will redevelop a picture that came out blurry or dark the first time to make sure that the flawed print was not their fault. While it is wonderful to have this kind of commitment to the development of your precious photos, there are also a number of convenient stores that will develop fine prints for a fraction of the cost.

The best deals for developing rolls of film are the warehouse stores and discount department stores. SAM'S CLUB takes up to three days, but a roll of double prints can cost as little as $3.49. Costco features similar prices for overnight development, but their one-hour costs can quickly add up. With any of these sources, it is recommended that you have a little patience and opt for the overnight prints. It is not as convenient, but waiting will save you a great deal of money in the end. If you are afraid to let your pictures off-site for overnight processing and decide to choose the one-hour processing options, be sure to look for coupons or discounts that will assist with the higher cost involved.

The discount department stores, such as K-Mart and Wal-Mart, have excellent prices on photo processing. Wal-Mart averages about $5.60 to develop a roll of double prints, and K-Mart has similar prices. Target charges $6.99 for next-day processing without a coupon, but many of their stores will include an index print. These stores also offer coupons and discounts. If you can catch any of these deals, the savings can be fabulous.

ALERT

Scrapbooking clubs sometimes hold "Scrappin' Yard Sales." These are events where scrapbooking addicts can sell seldom-used tools or materials in which they no longer have interest. Save money by purchasing the materials used, and if your club does not offer this, suggest it!

Specialty drug store chains such as CVS, RiteAid, or Eckerd Drugs sometimes have higher prices, but their convenient locations can make them an easier choice. It is important to not always count them out, as they sometimes offer good deals such as photo albums, free film, or double prints with every roll of film processed. These deals can be a great bargain, but be sure the "gift" is what you expect. Too many times customers have been disappointed because they were expecting a different size of print, a different speed of film, or a free gift that included a picture album made with archival quality materials.

Starter Kits

Another option you will find is the starter kit. These claim to contain everything you need to begin scrapbooking, and many kits do just that. The benefit of these kits is that true beginners can simply make one purchase and leave the store before they get overwhelmed. Many kits also contain instructions on how to get started. The downfall is that they are not really very good deals. Beginner or not, they force you to use a style that may not be your own.

Starter Kit
Cost

SCRAPBOOKING TOOLS	COST
Album	$19.99
100 sheets colored paper Pack (including white)	$2.99
5 pieces patterned paper	$.15 each: $0.75
1 set of letter stickers	$1.99
1 set of decorative stickers	$1.99
25 Pack Die-Cut Shapes	$1.99
1 Glue Stick Adhesive	$3.49
1 Pair of Edging Scissors	$5.99
TOTAL	**$39.18**

Recently, at a local scrapbooking store, a starter kit went on sale for $39.99 (most prices range from $49.99 to $69.99). It contained one 8.5" × 11" album, ten pages, ten pieces of color paper, five pieces of white paper, five pieces of patterned paper, one set of letter stickers, one set of decorative stickers, twelve die-cut shapes, one glue stick, and one pair of edging scissors. This may seem like a great deal because the items are exactly what you want to start with. But by walking around the store and collecting the same or comparable items and brands as those sold in the kit, it was easy to see that the quantity and sometimes also the quality of the individual items was much better. It's usually best to take the time to pick out your own materials and make sure you get exactly what you want, the best quality, and the most for your money.

Shop Around the Clock

The Internet is probably one of the best places to find discounts on all your scrapbooking materials. You will find that site after site offers specials on particular items, deals on item combinations (such as buy one item and get another for half off), clearance items, and shipping deals. They are very aware that many sites are now devoted to scrapbooking, and they keep very close tabs on one another.

FACTS

Scrapbooking magazines are expensive on the newsstand, but by subscription they are more affordable. *Creating Keepsakes* is $4.95 per issue, but a one-year subscription is $22.97. *Memory Makers* has a yearly subscription rate of $22.96, and *Paper Kuts* is $24.95. All magazines offer even better deals when you buy subscriptions for two or three years at a time.

Creating and Finding Discounts

The competition is so fierce that sites will sometimes offer you a discount simply to keep your business. One retail Web site responded immediately when they were contacted with the information that the complete set of alphabet punches they were selling for $119.99 cost only $99.99 on a competitor's site. It took no more than a day before the customer service representative emailed a coupon for 25 percent off—they were willing to give an extra $10 in savings simply to keep the business. This tactic does not work every time, but it never hurts to ask, either!

Time after time, you will find fabulous deals on the Internet by listening to peers on scrapbooking message boards. Checking these boards daily takes no time at all, and often it results in a bit of information that would have slipped past you had you not been aware of these knowledgeable resources (and friends). You will see posts such as "Great deal at ✐*www.dmarie.com*—I just found it! Specifics enclosed." Sharing these finds is truly a gift. They are just another reason among many to join a message board club.

Shipping Costs

Many sites will offer free or discounted shipping along with their already-low prices. Many sites offer year-round shipping deals, charging a small amount of money for larger orders. A couple of sites with nominal fees are ✐*www.gonescrappin.com,* which charges $1.50 for orders of $35 or more, and ✐*www.scrapbookutopia.com* which offers a $.99 shipping charge on almost all orders.

It is also important to consider weight when deciding which site will get your order. For example, ✐*www.creativexpress.com* has a flat rate of $4.75 per order. It would not be in your best interest to pay this much in shipping and order only ten sheets of, but that would be different if you wanted to order a heavy or large item that would normally come with an expensive shipping cost.

Join a Club

This is not your mother's women's club—scrapbooking clubs come in all shapes and sizes and will no doubt help save you money. The most popular clubs are regional, where groups of people with scrapbooking interests have formed an association for mutual enjoyment. They spend time together at crops, exchange tools, have contests, bring in speakers, and enjoy each other's company.

The cost for these clubs is usually minimal—some charge nothing and ask that everyone bring food or drink to meetings while others charge a small fee and put it towards refreshments, prizes, and tools. Some clubs charge a fee that goes toward the purchase of tools for the club. Anyone can use the club tools. For example, you might pay a $40 membership fee to join your club, but while cropping you can use the $60 embossing tool or the $120 set of alphabet punches that you normally would not have been able to afford.

ALERT

Scrapbooking clubs sometimes make you want to buy expensive tools that you cannot afford! It is easy to get caught up in the ease of some pricey items once you try them, but remember why you joined the club in the first place. Use the materials and tools offered by the club and spend your money elsewhere.

Another type of club is the virtual one. Message boards devoted to scrapbooking can be found on the Internet. These boards can seem intimidating at first, but please do not be turned off: Give them a chance! If you introduce yourself and discuss your interests, many people on the board—particularly the board leaders—will welcome you in no time.

Check out the message board for a few days (a practice known as "lurking") and get a feel for the board or club culture. Once you are ready, post an introduction in the morning so everyone will see it throughout the day. (The boards will usually archive each night, so posting in the evening might be useless.)

These makeshift clubs are a great way to save money. They conduct swaps for materials, carry out gift exchanges (called "secret scrappers"), offer each other store coupons, and post Internet coupons for anyone to use. They are usually the first place that Internet-based shopping specials are made known. Members have obtained countless money-saving ideas from these boards. You should not let a day go by without making a quick check. A great board to start at is ✍*www.parentsplace.com/messageboards.* Scroll down the list of boards to Crafts, and then Scrapbooking; you will not be disappointed!

Little Things Make a Big Difference

There are, of course, easy ways to look at your scrapbooking budget: compare prices, find sales, share items, and save! These are the most obvious, but let's not forget about all of the little things, the nitpicky ways to save a buck or two. These are not always as obvious as a 40-percent-off sticker, but added up they can really help out. Following are ten ways you can save a buck.

1. *Learn to find materials on the Web instead of in print.* The Web sites that are devoted to scrapbooking not only provide you with hundreds of options for shopping, they also offer a wealth of information and ideas. The Internet provides catchy and creative ways for scrappers to communicate their designs, such as a daily layout, weekly article, tool-of-the-month, and so on. The free items that are offered can and will save you from having to buy costly layouts, magazines with ideas, templates, etc. After all, why buy a magazine with a great pop-up layout idea when you can get it on the Internet for free?

2. *Make a list and check it twice!* How many times in your life have you been asked, "What do you want for your birthday?" or "What do you want for the holidays?" at the very moment that you actually know what you want? Probably never. It seems like some provision of Murphy's Law enables us to forget everything we have desired when we are asked these questions—and as luck would have it, it is only after the intended event that we remember. Start a wish list now so that when the special event comes you are armed and ready.

3. *Less is more.* In the chapters on creativity and layout, you will often hear that less is more. It's a common phrase that simply means that when you overdo a task, it often does not turn out exactly as you had intended. When you put too much on a page, you will frequently realize that it might have looked better without all of the accessories. Ask yourself whether you really need those stickers or that embossed paper to make the layout better. Do you have to have that patterned paper? Usually the answer is no, and with that simple reply comes the easiest of money-saving rules: simplicity.

4. *Make your own tools.* This does not mean that you need to break out your metal saw to create scissors or other major tools. Instead, it is recommended that you refrain from purchasing some plain tools that you can easily make yourself. You can easily make templates for basic shapes such as circles and squares with cardboard backings. Most of

the paper packs have these backings in them, so no purchases are necessary. Pencil around an object (a glass for circle, a coaster for a square, and so on) that you can find around your house. Then use an Exacto knife or scarp scissors to cut the template out. Finally, smooth the edges with a metal nail file. Other creative tools such as funky rulers or a light-box for stenciling can be made from simple household objects (such as waste lumber and window glass for a top).

5. *Attend free workshops.* Nobody ever said that you would know how to successfully scrapbook as soon as you bought your supplies. At the same time, though, this craft is not brain surgery. Having fun is one of our main objectives, and attending entertaining workshops can be a part of the pleasure. In budget terms, many of these workshops are free. Scrapbook stores or company consultants hold them with the intent that you will buy something from them. You may do just that, but please: Do not feel guilty if you choose to buy nothing at all! Attending these events is a great way to get ideas without having to spend money on costly classes or print materials.

6. *Give it a try.* Regretting a purchase is a terrible feeling, no matter the cost. Scrapbooking is a craft where we often get caught up in the idea of some special tool or interesting material, and we forget to stop to think about just how much we will use it. It seems almost glamorous to buy a set of twelve wavy scissors, but would you really use them? How about a stamping set of twenty-four stamps? Unless you are an avid stamper, you should think twice about whether you'll get your money's worth. Your best bet to save money is to give it the old college try. Borrow the tools, or buy just one to get acquainted with the material. Ask yourself these questions to figure out whether it is something you will use often: Is it a quality product? Could you use it in the future to swap for items that you do not have? Most important, is it worth the money? Only after all of these questions are answered to your satisfaction should you make the purchase.

7. *Organize.* Chapter 3 details the many reasons that organization is so important. One important purpose of organization is to save money. So often we forget about things we have purchased, only to find them months or years later (and frequently after we have purchased the

item again!). It is easy to buy holiday paper for a layout background only to find under a pile of supplies another set of holiday papers that you purchased from a clearance rack months before. Organization is an elementary but necessary step to saving money.

8. *Use every last scrap.* By using all of your materials, down to small scraps, you begin to save money on patterned paper, stickers, adhesives, as well as many others. For example, if you cut a 12" × 12" piece of patterned paper into as many circles as possible, you will be left with scraps of awkwardly shaped pieces. Instead of throwing these out, create small triangles or curves from these pieces and use them as an alternative to stickers. You can even place them on creative paper flowers. Another example is to use the letter outlines from letter sticker packets. Essentially you can use the frame of the letter. There are so many other ways to be creative with your leftovers, including using the extra from self-adhesives, creating a quilt background from your scraps, using sticker outline-frames, and so on. Throw materials in the garbage only when you are 100 percent confident that you will never need them again.

9. *Do not buy again until you have exhausted your supplies.* Many of us have more supplies than we will ever use, all because we did not use our current supplies before rushing out to purchase more. Buying for future events from a clearance rack is one thing, but buying an item simply because we "just have to have it" is another. Before you go to the store take a look at your supplies—if you are organized it will be very easy! Look through all of your papers, pens, and other materials that can be easily forgotten to make a mental note of the paper styles, ink colors, etc. Chances are you will save money by exhausting your current supplies before you splurge on new ones.

10. *Bring photos to the craft store.* It is so easy to go to the local scrapbooking store with the intention of buying supplies for one layout, only to be beckoned to buy other supplies you do not immediately need. If you bring the photos that you intend to use on a particular layout page, it is easy to remember why you went shopping in the first place. With this tactic, when you pick up something that you know will not be used in the layout, you can look at your pictures and recall the purpose of the trip.

Chapter 3

Systemize and Organize

I t's difficult to be successful with scrapbooking unless you organize. This chapter will offer tips on getting organized and present systems that have been successful to many involved in scrapbooking. You may decide to use these for your own organizational needs, or you might choose to draw on the ideas to help figure out your preferred method.

Get It All Together

To begin the diligent task of organization, there are three beginning steps that everyone needs to accomplish. Once these universal steps are complete, cataloguing and storing techniques will vary by personality and style.

1. Gather
2. Date
3. Pile

The first thing you need to do is gather everything you want to organize. Root through your attic or basement, and clean out old drawers. Set aside one room in your household that will be your home base for the project, and use it as a dumping ground for all of your materials and pictures.

Be aware that this step sometimes becomes a nice journey down memory lane, and it always lasts longer than you intended. Make sure that you put enough time aside to complete the job while at the same time taking a moment to enjoy these memories.

 **SSENTIALS**

This is a great time to go to your parents' houses and claim all the old high school and college memorabilia that they have probably been anxious for you to pick up. You may also find that it turns into a spring-cleaning of sorts: often these items are full of dust, so be sure to dress with the intent of getting dirty.

The second step is to create a personal time line in your life. You will certainly remember your spouse's thirtieth birthday party, or your fifteen-year anniversary trip—but if you were quizzed, could you easily remember the dates of these events? Most likely you would need some time to calculate dates from births, weddings, and so on. A personal time line will allow you to easily log photos and other items by year when you get to that step. For example, if you have a picture of your mother's forty-seventh birthday, you can easily figure out the year by looking at your personal time line to find out when she turned fifty. While figuring out these days without a personal time line would not be too difficult, creating one makes everything easier and faster. You can use this worksheet to help you get started.

Personal
Time Line
Worksheet

PERSONAL TIMELINE WORKSHEET

NAME: **DATE:**

Grandmother Born:

Grandfather Born:

Mother Born:

Father Born:

Birthday:

Kindergarten:

Religious Ceremonies:

6th Grade:

16th Birthday:

High School Graduation:

College:

College Graduation:

Travel:

Travel:

1st Job:

Engagement:

Wedding Day:

Ist Child Birthday:

   Kindergarten:

   Graduation:

   College:

   Wedding:

2nd Child Birthday:

   Kindergarten:

   Graduation:

   College:

   Wedding:

3rd Child Birthday:

   Kindergarten:

   Graduation:

   College:

   Wedding:

The final preliminary step in the organization of your memorabilia, pictures, and materials is to break them down into piles. It is effortless enough and an important step to creating a storage and organization system that you will use with ease. It depends on your personality and manner what you call each category, and, in turn, what each pile represents. Generally you will have some major sections: pictures, memorabilia, and scrapbook supplies. Within these sections is where you will create the your organizational style.

Categorizing Years of Photos

Once you are satisfied that you have created enough piles to start the detailed organization process, it is recommended that you begin by arranging the pictures. After all, you probably will not start scrapbooking until this is done, so organizing your scrapbook materials can wait until later.

It is important to ask yourself if you would prefer to view and locate your pictures by year or by event. You may prefer one or the other. Commence sorting as soon as you decide. A very orderly way is to use a combination of event and year, beginning with events. First, separate these pictures by major events. For example, you could stack them in the following piles:

- Holidays
- Birthdays
- Vacations
- School Pictures
- College
- Everyday Photos
- Major Events

Once you have your pictures broken down by category, it is important to go back to each subcategory and put them in order by year. This done, you will easily be able to find a picture when doing a particular subject. For example, if you wanted to complete a scrapbook layout that included both your college graduation pictures and your spouse's, it would be very easy to find them under "College." If you wanted to do a layout of all the major holidays in the year of 1975, you can look under your "Holidays" section and find the pictures from 1975 for each subsection.

Storing Your Photography

Now that you have your pictures arranged in an easy-to-find manner, it is time to put them in a storage container that is safe and easy to manage. A preference among scrapbookers is acid-free and safe photo storage boxes. These can be found in craft stores, photography stores, and on many Web sites. It is important to make sure that your photo storage box is archival quality. After all of this work, the last thing that you want to do is provide a container that could damage the prints.

Carefully examine the labels of photo boxes to determine that they are safe. Brands that claim to be "Photo Safe" may not be protected and could contain acid. Be sure to look for the terms "Archival Quality" or "Acid-Free" before you make your purchase.

Photo boxes are similar in shape, and often in size, to shoe boxes. For the sake of convenience, purchase a photo box for each of your major subjects. Within the box, break your pictures down by category and then by year. For each photo box and category, it is easy to use acid-free card stock cut into dividers with tabs. Label the box with the category and the card-stock tabs with the subcategory. As for the division of years, use acid-free index card-sized card stock labeled with the year and slip them in between your pictures.

Negative Storage Systems

Storing negatives with photos often results in clutter. One option is to use one photo-storage box for your negatives and break it down by major category (holidays, major events, and so on). Since double prints are available and recommended, the chances are slim that you will use negatives often. In the few cases that you do use them, it may take a few minutes to locate the exact negative, but your will be well spent in comparison to the time it would take to organize the negatives in the same manner as the photographs themselves.

Some scrappers store index prints with their negatives. If you are willing to spend it, the extra money may be worthwhile. Some processing plants even provide the index print free of charge. Generally, an index print will cost you between $1 and $3. It is also possible to bring old negatives to a processing center and have an index print made.

The Album Curse

As you begin the process of organizing photos, you will no doubt come across old albums of a type called "magnetic" or "sticky." They have sticky pages that can ruin a picture or piece of memorabilia in an instant. In performing rescue missions on material already stored in albums like these, the first order of business is to begin with the albums that are less than five years old. It is thought that the majority of damage to any photograph is done in the first five years: better to save recent photos than to tackle the project with photos that are already damaged to their fullest extent.

A good solution, albeit more expensive, is to take the picture as is, in the magnetic or sticky album, to a photography store and ask them to make a picture-of-a-picture. Some photocopy and drug stores also provide machines where you can do this process yourself for a nominal fee of $7 to $10.

As you begin to work your way though magnetic albums, you might find that some pictures are stuck and that taking them out would cause a tear and possible destruction. You can use dental floss to free your photos by gently sliding the floss back and forth behind a photograph until it becomes loose. Waxed floss works best because of the added lubrication it provides.

There are some other means of removing the photo if dental floss does not work. Tips ranging from a hair dryer to lighter fluid float around the Internet and even in some print materials. These forms of removal are not recommend as they will most likely ruin any chance you had of saving the picture. One product called Undo has a good reputation as an adhesive remover, but as with any chemical you put on your precious memories, try all other means first.

Surviving Catastrophe

The chances are slim that your photographs, negatives, or scrapbooks would survive a fire. Even in fireproof boxes that many of us keep for important documents, the heat will often cause negatives and pictures to melt. If you are worried about the safekeeping of your materials, or if you live in a highly insecure area prone to hurricanes or earthquakes, there are some precautions you can take.

Storing pictures or negatives in a safety deposit box is easiest because you know they will be protected. You can also put your photographs on a CD-ROM and place them into this storage system as well. Others make electronic scrapbooks and store them on the Internet. This is a good idea, but it will impose not only on your pocketbook but your time as well.

Cataloguing More Than Pictures

We all find memorabilia that we would like to use in our albums. These might range from wedding invitations to concert tickets, and they offer us even more memories than the pictures alone. Putting this type of memory into our scrapbooks requires us to make sure that the item is archived correctly and safely. A product called Archival Mist can do just that. Since materials like these are unstable until they are ready for use, a good method of storing them separately from pictures is to use an accordion filing system. These are often brown and have an elastic string that binds the book closed. Within the system you can create categories such as holidays, events, weddings, travels, school, and others.

Some people use storage systems for memorabilia that use large plastic tubs or containers. This is not recommended for one major reason alone: size. If you use a tub to store your scrapbooking items, chances are that you will begin to hoard objects that will never fit into a scrapbook. The logic behind any storage system is to make sure that we can easily find memorabilia that can be used in our scrapbooks.

Office-supply or home stores, not craft or scrapbooking stores, are the best place to find storage containers for items that are considered memorabilia. Accordion or other divider systems can be found in the file folder or the accounting section of these retail outlets.

A storage system that is too big will result in your placing items in it and allowing them to collect dust over the years. If your item cannot fit into an accordion-style system (or anything else you prefer that is of a similar size), chances are that it will not fit into your scrapbook. Your best course of action is to find another home for the item.

Storage Ideas for Scrapbook Supplies

There are so many materials that you can use for scrapbooks that it is easy to allow these materials to be buried underneath something else and forgotten. The orderliness of these items is significantly important to you in terms of both the money you save and your ability to keep yourself composed. Too many materials in an untidy space can be aggravating.

This type of organizing is subject to different personalities. There are only a few things that you need to keep in mind when putting a storage system together. These things will help you figure out what system is best for you.

1. Make sure you have easy access to your items.
2. Label everything. You will become so accustomed to looking at labels that if a section is not identified, you will likely skip over it.
3. Put all of the items that you use often in easy-to-reach places, as well as spaces that make it easy for you to put each item back. For example, if you have to dig underneath a few items for your scissors, chances are you will simply leave them on your desk. But if you kept these in a basket on your desk with other well used items, or in a convenient tote with open pockets, it is more likely that you will return them to their home immediately after use.

4. Write down what you have. Keep a master list of items and cross them off after they are gone.
5. Find a bag that will make it easy for you to transport materials.

Some ideas for storing your materials are listed below. Ranging in style and cost, they are ideas that have worked for others. You will come across countless ready-made storage systems at your local scrapbooking store or on the Internet. These work for some and are very convenient, but they can also be costly and may not exactly fit your own style. The ideas listed below offer alternatives to these manufactured systems.

FACTS

Paper was first invented in 4000 B.C. by the ancient Egyptians. Papyrus, a tall plant with a triangular thick stem, was a woven into mat of reeds and pounded into a hard, thin sheet. The word "paper" is derived from the word "papyrus." In A.D. 105, a Chinese court official mixed mulberry bark and hemp with water to create paper as we know it.

For storing your items, it is worth the money to buy plastic stacking cubes, hanging folders, wire bins, freezer bags, three-ring binders, and other similar storage tools. Some household items that are useful include empty diaper-wipe boxes, empty tissue boxes with an open box top (cut with scissors), and toolboxes. As with scrapbooking itself, there is no right or wrong solution to the problem of organizing your materials. As long as you have created a system that works for you, you will be off to a good start.

8.5" × 11" Paper

Organization methods for standard size paper are fairly easy. You can find good systems in any office supply store if you do not want to create your own. The nature of this popular paper size automatically gives you many options. One of the easiest systems is to use hanging folders in two colors (for sake of description we will use blue and yellow).

In the blue folders, arrange all of the plain colors in alphabetic order, providing a different hanging folder for each color. In the yellow folders, arrange your patterned papers into different hanging folders by categories such as plaids, romantic, holiday, template designs, and so on. Arrange papers within each of these categories by color as well (for example, group your red-based romantic patterns separately from your green-based holiday patterns).

12" × 12" Paper

The awkward size of this paper makes organization a bit more difficult than 8.5" × 11" paper. Several scrapbooking-oriented companies have created storage systems for this paper size. These are useful and often easier, but there are many other solutions if you do not want to spend the money on them.

Use a divider system that allows file folders to stand up in a holder instead of hanging. A holder system that holds folders in a descending stack will work best. Tabs will be hidden by the size of the paper, but since the paper can be easily seen in this system you won't really need labels anyway. Use different color file folders for plain and patterned paper. As with the 8.5" × 11" size paper, provide a new file for each plain color paper and organize in alphabetical order. The same can be done with the patterned paper, dividing it by category such as romantic, plaid, holiday, and so on.

Stickers, Die-Cuts, and Punches

Everyone has a particular way of organizing these tiny pieces of materials. That's important, because they can get away from you if not properly stored. Use a three-ring binder with see-through pouches that can close. The clear nature of these systems allows you to see everything you have, thus preventing much of the forgetfulness that we all suffer from now and then. It works best when you have one bag or sleeve for your stickers, another for die-cuts, and another for punch-outs. Depending on the amount of materials you have, you may need to divide these materials even further.

After recently participating in an alphabet-punch swap, it was easy to see that homemade storage systems worked best. Clear business-card holders that contain twelve slots per page can be easily found at local office-supply stores. Only two pages were needed, and each letter of the alphabet has its own case (assuming that X, Y, and Z share a space). These holders fit right onto a three-ring binder in with your die-cuts and stickers. They are a great way to make sure none of your letters get lost.

Storing pens vertically can cause premature drying of the ink or tips. Over long periods of time, be sure to place pens in a container or caddy that allows them to be stowed horizontally.

Scrapbook Tools

The best way to organize tools is to first break them down into two groups: frequent and infrequent use. This will allow you to put the tools that you use more often in closer proximity or easier reach than others. As with everything else, there are a number of ways to store these items.

The easier ones are systems that you can pick up and carry along. Two systems in particular, a toolbox or a plastic rubber box with a handle, seem to give scrappers more ease with transportation. Both are low-cost items that can be quickly put away or hidden in a closet. The portable file systems from office supply stores are the best; they tend to be compact but will still hold everything you need them to. Toolboxes are convenient because you can put seldom-used items in the bottom and reserve the removable tray for things you use a lot, such as adhesive, scissors, and pens.

If you do not want to spend any money on a storage system for tools, check around the house to see what can accommodate such materials. Do you have an old powder-room-sized wastebasket, or a milk crate that is not being used? If spending money on storage for your tools will prevent you from purchasing materials for your scrapbooks, be more creative in your storage process with household items. That way you can save the money to buy something you will treasure.

Punches, stamps, inks, and other bulky items might find a good home in shoebox-sized plastic boxes you can find in any dollar store or in discount department stores such as K-Mart or Wal-Mart. If these items exceed the storage of your everyday toolbox, you can use these plastic boxes for easy organization and still not spend too much money.

Using a small holder, such as a basket, near your workstation for your pens, frequently used scissors, glue-stick or other adhesives, and any other item you repeatedly look for can save you time and aggravation. You can quickly grab a tool every time you need to snip here or journal there, and it is as easy to replace as it was to find.

Tailor-Made Storage Systems

While shopping for materials on the Internet or in craft stores, you will no doubt come across systems that claim to be your answer to an organization nightmare. Many of these systems are excellent for particular uses, but that's also why problems arise. You might buy one of these supply cases only to realize that your uses differ from the specialty purpose that the holder was designed to fulfill. For example, you probably do not want to purchase a tote that can hold 8.5" × 11" paper if you frequently use 12" × 12". You can use many ideas in this chapter to make your own scrapbooking system, but there are excellent choices if you prefer. Ask yourself three questions before you purchase an organizing system:

- What materials do I use most while scrapbooking?
- What size paper and albums do I frequently use for scrapbooking?
- What do I need to take with me to crops or other scrapbooking events?

Once you have figured out what your needs are, choosing an organizational tool will take only a little more research. Go to Internet message boards and product review boards to find out what people are saying about particular items. The market for these systems is strong, and there are several brands that you will hear a lot about.

Styles of Storage Systems

Some popular styles of organizational systems are Cropper Hopper and Crop In Style. These have been successful by offering different styles of organizational systems to satisfy diverse needs. Popular items are the Roll Away Tote by Cropper Hopper, and The Navigator by Crop In Style. They are similar to the wheeled suitcases with adjustable handles. They are the most portable of systems and should have room for any kind of tool that you might have.

Before you buy, be sure to look at the quality of the item. Think about how much use it will get. If you plan on carting it with you a few times a week, it would be in your best interest to purchase a system that will weather the frequent use.

You will come across hundreds of other brands and styles of tote bags on the market. Once one brand offers a new style, look for competitors to offer rival designs.

Be Creative

In many discount department stores you will find items that are all-in-one storage systems. These are not necessarily for scrapbooking or any other crafts but instead are used frequently by college students, office managers, or in the home to store cleaning or other supplies. You can usually find them in a home storage section of these stores. Most have wheels so they can be easily pulled in and out of closets. Many of these systems contain a large bottom bin (or two) that will often hold 12" × 12" paper. Some have small drawers towards the top that can hold smaller materials like pens, scissors, punches, etc.

These systems can usually be had for a great price, somewhere between $20 and $40. If you have the money and storage space, they can save you some creative organizing on your own. Be sure to check the system out carefully; some are not made very well and can break easily. Also be inclined to purchase clear plastic systems instead of opaque colors—the better you can see your materials, the more you will use them. This will also prevent the need to label each door or drawer.

The Workstation

Beginning to scrapbook without a suitable workstation can get unruly. If your thought is to begin this project and then prepare an appropriate space, chances are that both you and the location you are using will become frustratingly disorganized. A scrapbook workstation should be:

- Free of clutter
- Within reach of your materials
- Out of the way of daily traffic
- Close to (or in) a location where children can play
- Easy to clean
- Well lit

It is most important that a workstation has a clean and level top. All of your supplies, with the exception of a basket or container of your most frequently used tools, should be in a location other than the desktop. These materials should, however, be within an arm's reach or at least very close.

The best workstations are out of the way of walkways and heavy traffic. They have surfaces and floors that are easy to clean or sweep. You will make a mess dropping scraps, adhesives, and other materials. Avoid areas with thick rugs where materials can get buried when choosing where to set up your workstation. Finally, since finding time is one of the biggest complaints of scrapbookers, a workstation in a play area will allow you to practice this craft while the children are occupied.

Lighting plays an important factor in the workstation. As with other crafts, scrapbooking becomes addicting. You might find yourself spending hours on your books. This work includes drawing, writing, tracing, and cutting. An area that is not well lit can be a strain on your eyes as well as your work.

Lighting also provides proper means of ensuring that the colors you have chosen for your layouts will actually be accurate! It is not enjoyable to walk into another room with better light and find that the colors on your finished page are not what you intended.

CHAPTER 4
Tools to Begin Scrapbooking

Aisles of tools lining the shelves of any craft store claim to be just the right thing to make your scrapbooking time well spent and easier. When making your first purchases, it is easy to feel besieged with the variety of tools at your disposal. Before you let the magnitude of materials available make you too dizzy, remember to take things one step at a time.

Album Variations

Albums are at the heart of scrapbooking. When starting out, it is easy to get overwhelmed by the large variety of options in albums. No matter what album variation you choose, you will require the same few basic qualities. These include acid-free and lignin-free pages, page protectors for keeping your work clean and undamaged, and something to ensure that all of the items you place into the book have been buffered for stability. There are five varieties of album bindings. Some are better for crafting a scrapbook than others, but the final decision is up to you.

Strap-Hinge Albums

Considered the most popular albums for true scrapbookers, the strap-hinge album has a flexible strap that runs through loops in each page. It is expandable, versatile, and the small separation between pages allows you plenty of freedom in designing two-page layout spreads.

 **E**SSENTIALS

To load pages into a strap-hinge album, first remove the spine from the album by sliding it out. Open the back of the album and unlace the straps. Once you have added pages, thread the straps through the staples on the hinge and into the album slots. Lace the straps through the hinge slots and cautiously pull the hinge straps until they are tight. Finally, replace the spine.

This album is easy to find in many sizes, including 8.5" × 11". Strap-hinge albums can be found in discount chain craft stores such as Michaels or Hobby Lobby. They can also be purchased from direct marketing companies like Creative Memories.

Ring-Bound Albums

Binders using a three-ring system or a five-ring system are also popular among scrapbooking enthusiasts. They are widely known as the easiest of books for scrapbooking, and for this reason beginners are often encouraged to use them. The ring binder system allows for pages to be added or transferred easily from one part of the binder to another. They also tend to have the most creative covers.

Ring binders costs range widely due to the large amounts of styles. Out of all of the different styles, however, the ring binders are the most cost-efficient. They are covered with standard paper or fabric, but many scrapbookers use the style to create their own stylish linen or padded decorative covers. Patterns for creating original covers can be found on the Internet.

The one major drawback and biggest complaint from all scrapbookers about ring binders is the impossibility of creating a flowing two-page layout in ring binders. Some try two-page designs only to be frustrated at the large rings that invade the path of the arranged design. Additionally, some complain about pages bending around the rings and destroying the layouts. Some of this can be avoided, however, by using a "D" style ring system, where the right side of the ring is a flat shape.

Post-Bound Albums

This classic style of memory album is not the most popular, it also has a timeless style. Its construction includes covers that are joined by metal posts. These posts can be extended to add additional pages to the scrapbook.

Post-bound albums can be purchased either from craft or scrap-booking stores or from direct sales companies such as Close To My Heart. The highest quality post-bound albums retail for about $40. After figuring in costs for card stock paper for layout pages, extender posts, and page protectors, a post-bound album might cost $60 or more. Some brands, including Generations, Pioneer, and Collected Memories, provide quality post-bound albums at reasonable prices.

Spiral-Bound Albums

Spiral bound albums are one of the two styles that have a set number of pages. They often have a hard cover and heavy card stock for the lay-out pages. Spiral-bound albums come in all shapes and sizes and are really in a class by themselves. They are sometimes not as durable as other styles, but because of their unique sizes and inexpensive cost, these albums can often become a favorite for gifts and small theme scrapbooks.

FACTS

The objects we use to collect pictures and memorabilia—which we know as an "album"—were originally tablets, not books, that the Romans used to record public edicts. An edict is a formal decree or proclamation issued by an authority and having the force of law.

The impossibility of adding pages with new layouts is often a turnoff for scrapbookers. It is also difficult to construct layouts in these albums since you have to work in the book, instead of on a page that can later be added or taken away.

Book-Bound Albums

Formal book-bound albums are durable and have the most classic look. Like spiral-bound albums, they cannot be expanded, but this fact is often overlooked in an effort to get the best and most durable book. Book-bound albums allow the pages to meet in the middle, thus permitting layouts with easy two-page designs. Since many of these books are used as heritage albums, the quality of the pages is often the same as paper used in museum and library collections. With some brands, an archival quality slipcover is included with the purchase.

One drawback is the cost—depending on the brand and quality, a book-bound album can cost $80 or more. Another problem is the difficulty of producing layouts that have layers or are bulky with textured materials. The lack of flexibility in binding constricts these materials and therefore will narrow your level of creativity. Book-bound albums are an excellent choice, but do not expect to use more than decorative paper, pictures, and journaling.

Album Size

The size of the album size you choose will affect everything related to scrapbooking. It is an important factor in your decision to buy. Too often, little thought goes into the size of the album and not until midway through the project (later than any of us would like) do you realize that the size is unsuitable for the current project. The larger the album, the more expensive materials and supplies become—not only with the book itself, but all of the scrapbooking accessories that go with it.

Before you make your decision on a size of scrapbook, consider the following questions.

- How many pictures do you plan to use per page?
- How much time do you have?
- Is cost a factor?

My, What Big Albums You Have!

Most people devoted to scrapbooking will tell you that they love their 12" × 12" albums. They are the most popular size and offer the greatest space for creating fun and interesting layouts. In everyday terms this is not a typical book size, but in scrapbooking 12" × 12" albums are a standard size. Because of their popularity, items correlating to 12" × 12" albums are common in direct sales companies, discount craft retail chains, and scrapbooking stores alike.

The biggest problems relating to the 12" × 12" size is the lack of continuity among scrapbooking suppliers. Albums that claim to be 12" × 12" usually contain pages that in actuality are up to half an inch off the mark on either side, which produces awkward results. If you are mixing and matching brands of patterned paper supplies, card stock, and album pages/brands, as many scrapbookers do, the differences in sizes can be irritating.

Some popular brands offer a 12" × 15" size album for scrapbooking enthusiasts. This is a big album dimension capable of presenting a large number of pictures and creative layouts. The problem that occurs most frequently is the lack of matching scrapbooking materials in the same size. It is not impossible, but it is difficult to find 12" × 15" card stock, colored paper, or patterned paper. Unlike awkward smaller-sized albums, papers cannot be cut to size in order to fit the page. They are simply too big.

Standard Issue

A standard size in paper and notebooks for business supplies is 8.5" × 11". This is probably one of the better sizes for anyone who is just starting out in scrapbooking. The small pages allow faster turnaround time from start to finish. They also make it easier for simplistic layouts to look full.

The biggest drawback to this standard size is the lack of space for highly crafted layout pages. Some complain that the pictures take up too much space, leaving no room for interesting borders, fun techniques, or big punch designs. While the 12" × 12" size does allow for more space, don't be fooled: with a little creativity, you can do anything you want on an 8.5" × 11" page.

One of the benefits of using standard sizes is the ease with which you can get materials. While only craft stores generally stock 12" × 12" scrapbooking items, any office-supply store stocks 8.5" × 11" paper, much of which is of archival quality. Crafters in more remote areas of the country, especially those with no access to online stores, prefer this to a long drive to the "local" scrapbooking store for materials in special sizes.

Small and Sassy

Smaller albums, including 5.5" × 8.5", 5" × 7", 6" × 8", and 6" × 6", are primarily offered in strap-hinge, post-bound, and most popular, spiral-bound albums. They are simple albums that call for modest layout and efforts, but they can also be beautiful, special, and great impression-makers.

FACTS

Petite albums are probably most commonly used as gifts. They can come as prefabricated pages only needing pictures to be added by the recipient or as completed books that journal good times and memories. These size albums take little time to create and can be much more special on that special occasion than a gift of a candle or picture frame.

Themes such as trips or special events are most often expressed in these sizes. They are perfect to take with you while traveling so you can create a scrapbook either as-you-go or on your return from a trip in order to create subject albums such as "The Grand Canyon." Theme albums of these sizes can be extra special. They are also a bit more distinctive than four pages of a 12" × 12" album of the same event.

Album Accessories

Alongside the scrapbooking album section in any craft store, you will no doubt see countless items that relate to the scrapbook. Some of these are a necessity if you are serious about maintaining archival quality materials. Album accessories range in price, getting more expensive as the albums get larger in size.

Page Protectors

A page protector is an archival quality plastic sleeve that fits over your scrapbook page for protection. These can be found to fit pages in any standard size of scrapbook album. The sleeves have a high gloss, but sometimes for a little extra money you can find them in a non-glare style. This accessory comes in either side- or top-loading styles, both of which are fairly easy to use. Most are sold in packs of ten or fifteen, with prices ranging from $5 to $12 depending on the size and brand.

One mistake to avoid is the purchase of a particular size page protector to fit your album page without figuring in the style of the album itself. Page protectors made for a 12" × 12" album in a strap-hinge format will most likely not fit a post-bound page, and vice versa.

Refills

Strap-hinge, post-bound, and ring-binder album styles all allow you to add more pages to them. Refills for these albums are common, and most can be found on the same shelf as the album itself in a scrapbooking store.

It is important to know of the maximum number of pages that your album can hold. For example, in most strap-hinge albums, fifteen pages are included with your original purchase. It is recommended that you use no more than thirty-five or forty-five pages, or about two refill packages. Keep in mind too the amount of materials you have adhered to each page. A scrapbooker who uses heavier materials will probably want to use fewer refill pages in the album. Overloading an album can mean breaking the spine or binding.

Covers and Imprints

The appearance of the cover of an album is especially important to some. While most come in pleasant fabrics, leathers, or papers, there are some enthusiasts who prefer to create covers of their own. If you want to create a fabric-cushioned cover, you can often find patterns to assist you in craft stores or on the Internet. Special covers for paper albums, usually in the spiral style, can include quotes or an introduction to the book.

Homemade cover of a friendship album

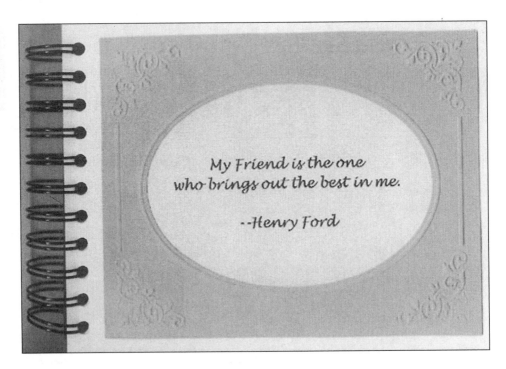

My Friend is the one who brings out the best in me.

--Henry Ford

Many who spend the money on book-bound albums are also willing to pay for imprinting. This is a classic look. A leather-bound book is inscribed with a gold or silver mark. It is usually very simple, stating the name or the year and event. Imprinting in this manner comes at a cost, and prices vary. It is best to contact your local printing store for exact charges.

ESSENTIALS

Reviews of many brands of basic tools can be found on the Web site ✍ *www.scrapbookaddict.com/reviews*. Reviews and statements from users of brand-name albums, scissors, adhesives, plus many other items are organized in an easy-to-read system. You can look at specific written reviews, or use the overall rating to help you make a purchasing decision.

Please Pass the Paper

Paper comes in all shapes and sizes, and having a nice collection of diverse colors and patterns will make your craft much easier. As you shop around, you will find that paper comes in many different thicknesses, hundreds of brands, and in colors you probably never anticipated you would use in a scrapbook. Eventually you will probably find a brand that you prefer because of quality or style, but in the meantime it is important to understand all of the differences.

FACTS

Paper and cardstock density is measured in terms of thickness. Sizes for some standard materials include the following: Copy Paper: .004", Lightweight Cardstock: .008", Business Cards: .01", Cereal Boxes: .02", and Milk Carton: .125".

Paper comes in many weights and thickness, termed "paper grade." This categorization of distinct styles of paper is based on the type of pulp, treatments, and end use. Some examples are bond paper and newsprint. For scrapbooking purposes, card stock is the most common grade of paper. It is essential that all the paper you use for scrapbooking is acid- and lignin-free.

For the beginner, variety packs of paper can be an easy way to build up your on-hand supply. Purchase a pack of paper in the size of your album, as well as an extra pack of 8.5" × 11" for mounting pictures, etc.

Variety packs can be purchased in themes such as primary colors, pastels, or dark colors. Stock up on these and make note of the colors you prefer. Often, they will reflect your own personality. Most important, never throw away a color because you think it is not flattering. You will be surprised at how an ugly shade of purple can be inspiring and look fabulous in the right layout!

Patterned Paper Pleasures

Decorative papers adorned with both simple and active designs can be found lining many scrapbooking and craft-stores shelve. Online stores, catalogs, and craft chains boast about the numbers of patterned styles they carry, with as many as 3,000 styles on display at one time. Unlike other materials, most scrapbookers do not tend to prefer any one brand of paper over any other. They simply look for patterns that will complement their layouts.

Patterns can completely change the look of your layouts. It is important not to let busy paper detract from your pictures. Most patterned papers are well done and can completely accent your designs. For example, light blue paper with clouds is perfect for a sleeping-baby spread, and red-and-white checkered paper can perfectly complement a barbecue layout. Some designs may not be suitable for use alone or as an entire background, but used in punches, cut into borders, or as a background for mounting pictures, they can add just the right touch.

Textured Papers

Some papers will have different textures, such as mulberry or even faux suede. Mulberry, one of the trendier papers, has a wonderful natural look for a layout with an unrefined appearance. It can be used to mat photos or with its edges torn can add a wispy expression to your artwork.

Voluptuous Vellum

A translucent paper called vellum has become very popular with scrapbooking enthusiasts. It can be found in many colors including clear (or milky), as well as simple patterns and designs. New styles of vellums, including alphabet letters and die-cuts, are found in stores daily.

Vellum can be used to make very creative pages. Due to its clear nature, it has a great look for matting pictures. It can be used in journaling, both atop busy paper for a muting effect and on darker paper for a foggy look. Use caution with the type of pen you use to journal on vellum. Inks take longer to dry on this material and can easily smear. Also, be sure the adhesive you use dries clear. Since this is a translucent paper, clear glues are an absolute necessity.

FACTS

Use mulberry and vellum papers when creating a snow scene or winter layout. Mounds of snow can be created by wetting a cotton swab and using the tip to draw uneven hills on white mulberry paper. Tear the paper on the damp line. Do this a few times and layer the snow mounds to create a three-dimensional look. Use punches to cut the vellum into snowflakes to finish off this creative but simple layout.

Some vellum papers are not archival quality and are unsuitable for long-term use in albums. Archival quality paper is treated with calcium carbonate to make it opaque. The translucent effect that vellum is praised for also is also an indication that this treatment step might not have taken place. Check carefully for an acid- and lignin-free stamp on the vellum product you purchase.

Most scrapbookers use vellum for cutouts such as clouds, raindrops, snowflakes, swimming pools, or bath bubbles. Some of the most creative uses of vellum include using it to portray drinking/champagne glasses, angel or fairy wings, and windows. You can even emboss jagged edges to create flames.

Pen Pals

Unlike paper, where variety increases the possibilities for personal expression, the thousands of varieties of pens on the market can be more of a bother than a convenience. Choosing a pen becomes difficult mostly due to personal preferences and styles of handwriting. Because of the expense, it is important to get it right the first time.

One of the more creative pens on the market includes a style that lets you write directly on card stock to create a watermark effect, producing letters that are slightly raised and the same color as the paper but in a darker shade.

When selecting a pen to use in scrapbooking, it is first important it meets your standards for scrapbooking purposes. Pens must be permanent, fade-resistant, photo-safe, and waterproof. It is also helpful to have quick-drying pens that will not smear as much when you journal on paper or vellum. As always, all pens must be acid-free and nontoxic.

Ink colors come in every shade and hue imaginable. Most companies provide storage cases for craft stores that easily display this large variety to ensure that you will not miss the color you want. Be careful not to depend on the cap color when making your decision. If at all possible, scribble on some paper to make sure it is the color you are looking for. Starting with the basic colors is always the best, but once you are comfortable using different pens, it is easy to enhance your creativity with gel glitter pens, metallic paint pens, and other unique styles to add a fun touch to your pages.

Left-handers beware! Do not allow a right-handed person to borrow your felt tip pens! Left- and right-handed people press the tip of a pen in opposite directions. If weight is put onto your pen from someone who writes with the other hand, your pen tip could fray, streak, or even break.

Styles of pens range from gel-rollers to calligraphy, fine-point to broad-tip. Pens used for journaling usually are in the fine-point variety, ranging in tip width from .001 to 1.0, averaging at .05. Once you increase the tip size to above 1.0, pens can be used to outline letter headings or make captions. Some pens do not post the size of the pen head, simply stating "fine" or "broad." These pens are worth using, but be sure to try it first as one company's definition of "fine" might be different than another.

Pens that have special tips can help you be very creative with your lettering. Brush-tips are artistic markers that feel like a small paintbrush. Some use this pen for crafted, flowing letters, while others use it to easily fill in block lettering or other inventive creations. Calligraphy tips are cut straight at the end to allow for ease in creating script letters. These also come in different sizes. As always, it is best to try the different sizes before you make your purchase.

Adhesives: A Sticky Subject

Mounting your pictures, souvenirs, or layouts is an integral part of scrapbooking. It should therefore come as no surprise that there are many styles and brands of adhesives on the market. The type of adhesive you use will depend on the styles of layouts you most often produce.

One important factor to keep in mind when deciding on an adhesive is making sure that it is permanent, acid-free, and nontoxic. The best advice from scrapbookers is to keep plenty of adhesives on hand. Adhesives can fall into two primary categories: liquid and solid. You will need at least one of each category when scrapbooking.

Liquid Adhesives

Glues that are in a concentrated form can be called liquid. They include glue pens, glue sticks, and bottled glues. Liquid adhesives are used primarily on items that have awkward shapes or needed for adhering small areas.

Glue pens are the most versatile style. They have a wide range of tip sizes that allow you to apply a simple dot or a long line of glue. Glue sticks are also easy to use, but not as dependable as pens. The glue dries very quickly, sometimes so fast that you do not have a chance to adhere the paper or picture. To combat this, some manufacturers have created a glue that is blue when wet but that dries invisible. It comes in both a glue stick and glue pen form.

Solid Adhesives

Solid adhesives can usually be found in some form of two-sided tape. This style is great for fastening large papers and pictures. The primary difference is in the styles of dispensers that hold the tape.

Tape rollers allow you to apply a double-sided tape by rolling it across the item with the dispenser. Photo Splits are applicators that administer precut portions of double-sided tape. Some dispensers contain tape with peel-off backings that will allow you to apply the adhesive but only use it when you are ready for the layout. The last style is Photo Tape. This is similar to the Photo Split, but it does not come in precut tabs, meaning you can decide how small or how big you want the portion of tape.

FACTS

Un-Du is a liquid adhesive remover that is safe to use in scrapbooks. The product comes with a lifting tool that aids you as the drops are poured onto the unwanted item. The spot of liquid evaporates quickly and disappears on the page. It even allows you to reuse stickers or die-cuts that were removed with the product.

An alternative to solid adhesives is sticky dots. These can be found in large sheets. They are used for awkwardly sized items, punches, and die-cuts. They work a little differently from other adhesives. You firmly affix the die-cut to the sticky dot sheet and then carefully remove it. The die-cut will now contain double-sided sticky dots on the back. and is ready for mounting in your layout. This is an excellent option for intricate shapes.

Adhesive Alternatives

Aside from these categories, we also find many adhesive styles that can be useful and decorative at the same time. Photo corners are a type of adhesive that fastens pictures without adhering glue to the picture itself. A photo corner is a 90-degree sleeve pouch that fits on the corner of the photo.

The back of this contains adhesive, and this is affixed to the scrapbook page. Another alternative is a mounting pouch, a small clear sleeve that contains one line of adhesive at the top. These are often used to collect items that are difficult to secure, such as a lock from baby's first haircut.

A few expensive but popular adhesive products are found at scrapbooking stores. Machines that produce adhesives on the back of die-cuts, paper, and pictures are a hot trend at the moment. Owners are thrilled with the power to create stickers out of items that might have once have been difficult to adhere, such as letters or awkwardly shaped clip art. If you have the money, it is a marvelous tool. These machines can also laminate or create magnets, but beware that the heat from some of these special features can damage your items.

A Cut Above the Rest

There is an enormous variety of cutting materials, all of which can be helpful in scrapbooking. Many of these will be discussed in the next chapter. For your basic tools, all you need to get started is a good pair of scissors.

Find a pair of high-quality straight-edged scissors that can assist you with cutting paper and cropping pictures. Make sure they are comfortable with your grip and are lightweight. A good pair of scissors will come with a manufacturer's warranty and have a secure tension.

A couple of sizes of scissors can help, but they are not necessary. If you can get more than one pair, opt for a pair of micro-tip scissors that can easily cut small corners and edges. All of your scissors should have blade tips that meet at the edge points.

Keeping your scissors sharp is also important. Test for sharpness by cutting thick paper in small and intricate edges like a small star. If they need sharpening, a home remedy is to try cutting them through sandpaper or aluminum foil a few times. Some companies offer a scissors sharpener that works well, and some craft stores have sharpeners on hand.

If you need to loosen the scissors, try a little oil, but be sure to clean the scissors thoroughly before you use them. Finally, try not to drop your scissors! Hard falls can cause these tools to shift alignment.

CHAPTER 5

Beyond Basic Tools

O nce you have the basic necessities and are comfortable moving forward, the styles of scrapbooking tools that are available are tremendous. This chapter is a synopsis and explanation of what you will find at the local craft store to help you figure out what tools are best for your scrapbooking needs.

Cutting Systems

Creating circles, ovals, and even straight lines normally takes a steady hand and a lot of concentration. One bump can make the biggest difference, and it feels like the more we try to correct cutting mistakes with our handheld scissors, the more obvious the mistakes become. Companies producing craft tools recognized this problem and created an entire stock of cutting systems to assist our cutting error nightmares.

Steel blades rust very quickly in humid areas. Fine sandpaper can get rid of rust spots on your blades. Keep plenty on hand in case the rust prevents a clean sweeping cut.

For all cutting systems, it is important to work on a clean and level work surface. Make sure that you have enough room and that other materials are out of the way. Even though most come with protective safety features, the main element of a cutting system is the blade, so keep focused on what you are doing.

State-of-the-Art Cutters

Circle and oval cutting systems are engineered products that allow you to create a shape without using handheld scissors. They vary in level of complexity, but most are easy to operate as long as you read the instructions carefully.

Some popular companies that make and sell quality cutting tools include Accu-Cut, at ✐ *www.accucut.com*, Coluzzle, at ✐ *www.coluzzle.com*, and Fiskars, at ✐ *www.fiskars.com*.

As with all cutting systems, it is important that your blades remain sharp to ensure a smooth cut. Blades can easily get dull, and they are not expensive to replace. Pliers are the best tools to assist replacing a blade. Your system will come with instructions on how to make the change.

The base of the cutting system should be a nonslip surface. Most glass bases have slip-preventative materials on the bottom, often called gripper feet. Visit any hardware store to purchase rubber feet at a low cost for an easy way to fix bases not equipped with this safety feature.

Be sure to check that the system is level after you adhere the gripper feet. One household item that can help with slippage is gripper lining, the kind that is placed under a rug to prevent slipping on a hardwood floor. Cut a piece as big as your base and affix it with glue.

Swivel-Knife Systems

There are a number of specialized cutting systems on the market. They come in template forms accompanied by a swivel knife and cutting board. These devices are economical and can be found in the scissors section of most stores, but they do take practice before you use them on your pictures.

Systems like the Coluzzle Cutting System or Accu-Cut's Shapemakers Tools are made of transparent plastic templates. Within the templates are shapes, including basic circles and ovals, alphabet letters, puzzle pieces, and detailed figures. The shapes come in varying nested sizes, held together by a simple bridge. By layering the shapes, it allows for ease in cutting a mat for a picture or backdrop for a design.

Before using a template cutting system, make sure the plastic film gripping the template on both sides is peeled away. Additionally, the bridge holding the nested shapes in place should never be cut.

The template systems use specialty swivel knives and mats that are included in the original purchase. Many use this system because the only requirement is to keep your wrist in one position while cutting. There is no "steering" when cutting the shapes, and the template track guides the swivel knife with little exertion.

Personal Trimmers

Remember paper cutters in grade school? As it turns out, these little gadgets are great for scrapbooking. Personal trimmers come in sizes ranging from 7 to 20 inches. You will find them in two types: arm blade and sliding blade.

A 7-inch personal trimmer is lightweight, easily transported to crops, and great for cutting pictures in a straight line. Its size, however, does prevent larger pieces of paper from being cut at one time. Most scrappers prefer a 12-inch version of the personal trimmer. They can cut a piece of 12-inch paper straight with no worries of ruining expensive patterns.

Rotary Cutters

Often used by quilt-makers, rotary cutters look a lot like pizza cutters. Use them by placing a ruler on top of the material you would like to cut. Roll the blade along the straight edge. With one hand, place pressure on the ruler while cutting with the other.

FACTS

A red-eye reduction pen is a specialized scrapbooking tool that uses a translucent ink to create a natural-looking eye. Use of this tool allows scrappers to use pictures not originally thought of as scrapbook-quality.

Cutting mats are especially important for rotary cutters. The more pressure you exert on the rotating blade, the more your surface can be damaged if it is not properly protected. It is recommended for ease and accuracy that you stand while using a rotary cutter. Additionally, rotary cutters frequently have replacement parts that include decorative paper edgers.

Decorative Scissors

Decorative scissors are shaped in fun and creative designs that can accent your pages beautifully. They come in all shapes and sizes, ranging from a tiny scallop to more interesting styles such as Fiskars Brand Alligator or CorkScrew. They are a pleasant change, and can even be flipped, which results in a backward cut and a completely different style.

Purchasing these edging pieces, more than anything else, can be addictive. Be careful: As many scrapbookers will tell you, it is easy to become collectors of these items but not users.

Examples of decorative scissor cuts

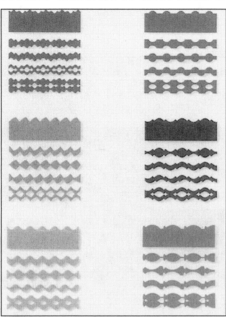

If you do use decorative scissors, these tools can make for some stylish layouts and assist in everything from heritage to children's albums. Fiskars Brand makes a classic pack of its original six styles. This is a great way to start and decide whether it would be worthwhile to buy other patterns. The classic-pack retails for about $30, but a little searching on the Internet will probably turn up less expensive prices. Individually, quality decorative scissors range in price from about $4 to $8 each.

Some of the most popular uses of these tools are to create accent photo mats, decorate corners, or produce fashionable borders. If you get even more imaginative, the uses for them are endless—funky letters, creative Easter eggs, ocean waves, leaves for trees, and much more.

Think carefully before you cut precious photos with decorative tools. Some heritage photos or other pictures that do not have negatives are irreplaceable. Reconsider using creative edging on mounting materials such as patterned paper.

Punch 'Em Out

Paper punches are available in an assortment of shapes and sizes, from small hearts to large snowflakes. Punch art is a technique that results from paper punches. It is described in detail in Chapter 12. They work in the same fashion as a typical hole-punch, inserting the paper into the punch and pressing to create the design.

Some brands offer a punch system, allowing you to insert different styles of punches into the punch mechanism. These are worthwhile if you find that punch art is a style you want to pursue in your layouts. Due to the expense, it is recommended that you buy one or two punches to start with, and see if these tools can assist your scrapbooking needs. You can also borrow a punch for a few days from a scrapbooking club or a friend.

Examples of craft punches

Punches can become fickle, hard to operate, and sometimes even hurt your palm when you press. If a punch sticks, slice it through wax paper a few times. Sometimes this small lubrication can be a lifesaver. If this doesn't work, try taking it apart and putting it back together. This should be a last resort, and you have to be careful and meticulous in remembering where everything goes. This step, however, works almost every time. Quite often the pesky punches go out of alignment, and a simple retooling can save the day.

Craft Punches

Craft punches have creative shapes that allow you to dress your page in interesting arrangements. The standard shapes include hearts, stars, circles, squares, and so on. As you use your shapes more, it will be fun to use some other distinctive styles like spirals, leaves, and footprints.

The Crucial Corner Rounder

Many scrapbooking enthusiasts believe the corner rounder to be the best invention for this craft. Its name speaks for itself, it rounds the corners of scrapbooking materials, primarily photographs. The outcome reminds us of the classic way we used to receive photographs from the processing center.

 **ESSENTIALS**

If your decorative scissors or paper punches are dull, try cutting them through fine sandpaper or aluminum foil a few times. It usually generates a small enough improvement to aid in finishing your layout page.

This is such a popular product that it is often put in a category by itself. But make no mistake, this too is a punch. Working the punch is easy as well. You simply slide the corner of the photo or paper into the punch and press down. It will result in four corners that are equal in the depth of the curve.

Corner Punch Patterns

Corner punches are becoming some of the more popular items in scrapbooking. They come in all kinds of designs that include scallops, hearts, and stars. Some of the designs look ornamental in their structure and are a favorite for heritage pages.

Using photo
corners to
mount
pictures

Corner punches let you mount your photographs without using glue. These corner punches, also known as photo corners, cut the mounting paper to make a slot for the photo corner to slip through. This is a great way to protect your photographs while at the same time, adding a decorative element to your scrapbook page. It is also a terrific alternative to traditional photo corners that have adhesive backings.

Die-Cut Fundamentals

Die-cuts are synonymous with scrapbooking. They are shapes cut by a die-cut machine using a particular paper or ink. They are used in most scrapbooks at one time or another. Die-cuts assist in embellishing a page and creating beautiful layouts.

QUESTIONS?

How many sheets of paper can I use in a die-cut machine at one time?
Die-cut machines can normally handle up to five pieces of paper at one time, or about the thickness of a piece of poster board. If you create more than one die-cut, ask the store to buy leftovers to resell to customers.

Many scrappers purchase prefabricated die-cuts from scrapbooking or craft stores. These are easy to obtain, often coming in theme packs. For example, you can purchase a cowboy theme of die-cuts that will include a sheriff's badge, a cowboy boot, and a lasso. They can also be purchased individually, generally for between $.18 to $.25 each.

Buying premade die-cuts is easy, but creating them is more fun. Local scrapbooking stores and educational institutions are the best places to find a die-cut machine. The machines are smaller than you would think, and they are easy to operate. Of the two styles of die-cut machines available, roller or lever, the lever system is more popular and can often be found in independent stores.

It is important to read the instructions on using a lever die-cut machine and to ask for assistance the first time you try it out. Generally, however, the machines can be used by following these simple steps:

1. Place paper against the rubber face of the die.
2. Raise the lever handle of the machine.
3. Slide die and paper into the machine, wooden side facing up.
4. Make sure the die is flush with the back.
5. Carefully bring the handle down.
6. Gingerly raise the handle—most will swiftly and dangerously swing back if you let go.

To use a portable die-cut machine at an independent scrapbooking store, conduct yourself with respect for the store and storeowner. Make sure you contact the store to see if there is a set schedule, a time limit, or if reservations need to be made. Once you are at the store, ask for directions and assistance the first time you use the machine. Store workers can be particularly helpful with ideas on paper conservation and machine tips. Finally, put all of your dies away and make sure the area is clean for the next user.

Sticker Paradise

Stickers are more than just a toy for children; they can also be a very influential piece of scrapbook art. There are hundreds of companies that create stickers, and this is the tool where "archival quality" can easily be forgotten. Look for the acid-free label before making your sticker purchase.

Stickers can be acquired as a collection or theme. Basically, you will buy a pack of stickers that has a variety of designs including baby, floral, vacation, beach, sports, wedding, holiday, teddy bear, cartoon characters, and many more. So refreshing sometimes, stickers can be a catalyst to an entire layout. There are many times when scrapbookers base a whole page on one set of stickers that they found.

Using stickers
to decorate
a title

The variety of ideas that results from stickers is tremendous. They can be used for layout borders, page breaks, or corner embellishments. Drawing from photos, they can surround or complement one area of the picture. Carefully placed stickers can cover mistakes on your layout pages, and interesting sticker combinations can create an entire scene. Additionally, stickers can decorate lettering and gracefully adorn a title or caption. Truly, the possibilities are endless.

FACTS

To format your sticker-letters into a layout, first space your letters evenly over the page with a pencil. Using a pair of tweezers, place your letters onto the page. Wait until all of the letters are arranged to your satisfaction before firmly pressing the adhesive onto the scrapbook page.

Most popular are letter-stickers. Numerous fonts are used to create these easy-to-use alternatives to personally lettering titles or captions. The alphabet usually comes with three sets of frequently used letters, along with numbers and punctuation marks. They also come in both upper- and lower-case packages. Using sticker letters will save you a lot of time, but remember: the smaller the sticker, the more difficult it is to manage.

Templates and Rulers

Templates are a practical alternative to costly circle and oval cutting systems. The most common templates are basic shapes including hearts, squares, and rectangles. Templates usually are packaged with the template cutout still attached. Do not throw these out because you may find them useful in the future.

Many templates provide you with numbers that correspond to the size of the cutout, increasing in number as the sizes increase. This is helpful for layouts that include mounting a picture onto a piece of paper. For example, if you wanted to mount a photo that you cut using the #4 template rectangle, you would then use the number 5 or 6 template rectangle to cut the background. This system makes for easy measuring and few headaches.

Lifting a template after tracing a design with ink can smear on the page! Try putting a small piece of thick material underneath the template to raise it a little and prevent smearing when you lift it up.

Designer Templates

Some templates come in interesting shapes including dolls, hats, trees, and so on. Others are decorative curvy lines that are used to dress up a picture placement or page break. Using these are fun and a good alternative to die-cuts, clip art, or punches. The template cut out of paper can be used as a backing for photos, a decoration for the page, or an area to provide journaling.

Lettering is a popular use for templates. The alphabet can be found in ready-made templates in both upper and lower cases. Tracing or stenciling the letters onto your paper or card stock is easy work and can create great layouts. This is a good alternative to lettering on your own, but it can be tedious and time consuming if you decide to cut out each stenciled letter. While this is a great look, save it for large, plump lettering templates where you will have little or no intricate angles.

Fancy Rulers

Using fancy rulers and stencils to decorate a page

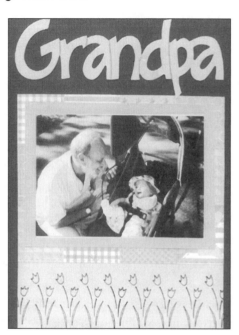

Ornamental rulers are good tools to use for borders and page breaks. They help you create a flowing look that freehand might have muddled. Rulers can come with one decorative edge and one straight edge, or with two decorative edges and some template designs in the middle.

A favorite among scrappers are L-shaped decorative rulers. These often have an outer edge of embellishment and an inside straight-edge. They are the perfect tools for adorning layout page corners. Additionally, these L-shaped templates have a lot of smaller designs within the clear plastic template including flowers, trees, houses, numbers, letters, and so on. These are easier to carry with you to a crop than bulky punches that can create equivalent designs.

The Light-Box

A light-box is a tool that is used to re-create images on a piece of paper for use in your scrapbook. It has a clear top that is placed above a light source. The idea is to place your image on the clear top and then place the paper on which you wish to trace it above the image. The light will allow you to see the image and easily trace it. This is often done when you find a design that you love that you need to re-create it because it is in a book or not printed on archival quality material.

A basic light-box can cost between $30 to $60 from a craft store. There are, however, numerous household objects that work fine as light-box substitutes, or you can easily make one of your own.

Some items around the house that can supply you with a light-box include glass-topped coffee tables or windows. One of the best items is a round side-table that has a glass top. These are often covered with a round decorative tablecloth. When you remove the cloth and glass top, you will most likely find a pressed wood tabletop with a large hole in the middle. Put a small lamp underneath the uncovered table and replace the glass. Not only is this a creative way to make a light-box, it is very convenient. You can simply pull up a chair and go to work.

If you are you handy, making a light-box out of scrap wood and Plexiglas materials is easy. The best size is 16" × 16" to accommodate papers that are up to 12" × 15". Follow these simple instructions.

Light-box instructions

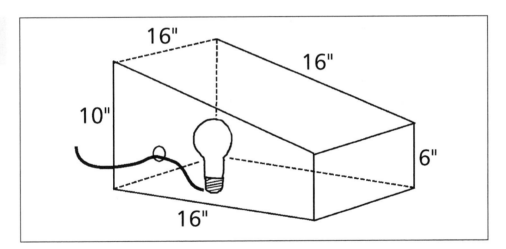

Materials:
- 1 light-box back, wood ¼" thick, 16½" × 10½"
- 1 light-box front, wood ¼" thick, 16½" × 6½"
- 1 light-box top, plexiglass, 16" × 16"
- 2 light-box sides, wood ¼" thick, 10" (at the back) × 16" (along the top and bottom) × 6" (at the front), see diagram

- 12 wood screws
- drill
- light source
- light bulb

Instructions:

- Using 2 wood screws on each side through the back, connect the light-box with each side.
- Using 2 wood screws on each side through the front, connect the light-box with each side.
- Using 2 screws on each side, connect the Plexiglas top with the angled box.
- Drill a small hole in the back and connect a light source (available at any home supply store).

Using Technology in Scrapbooking

Aside from the obvious Internet resources, other handy computer-related items include software programs and clip art. Scrapbookers that use computers and photocopiers swear by the ease of these tools and often encourage others to jump on the bandwagon.

SSENTIALS

When using any kind of technology to find items for your scrapbook, it is important to keep in mind the golden rule of safety. Where will you print out your items, and are the inks and papers acid-free? Find the answers to these simple questions before printing out your clip art or lettering.

Photocopy Phenomenon

Photocopiers are one of the easier tools to work with in scrapbooking. They can completely change the look of a page by allowing you to enlarge a picture, duplicate a design, reverse images, or print on colored paper.

The toner in photocopiers is generally considered safe for scrapbooks. Make sure the paper in the machine is acid-free. If you add your own paper, check that it is in the correct tray. If in doubt as to the safety of the materials, perform an acid-free test to be sure.

Laser and Ink Jet Printers

The biggest obstacle when using a printer is the ink. If using a laser printer, the chances are that the toner, a similar substance to photocopiers, is acid-free. Ink Jet printers, on the other hand, may be somewhat acidic, although often not in high enough levels to cause alarm. It is always best to check with the manufacturer before permanently placing these items in your scrapbook. Designs printed with thick patches of ink also have a tendency to chip if removed too quickly from the machine or if the page bends an awkward way.

There have been no conclusive studies on the permanence of printer ink, and it is a concern. Most manufacturers have statements about their products in the packaging or on the company Web site, and often there are only a few printers in a company line that do not have acid-free ink. They also have testimonials about the inks fading over time and other safety issues. When you purchase or use a printer for producing images for your pages, adhere to a few simple rules:

- Print on acid-free paper or card stock.
- Keep printed material away from water.
- Color printed clip art with acid-free pencils and pens.
- Use page protectors.
- Store in a dark area.

Computer Journaling and Lettering

There are a couple of standard methods to using a basic word program for journaling. An easy way to use this feature is to simply type the text, choose a font, and print it out in a paragraph form. In a similar manner to clip art, cut out the text and adhere it to your layout. The second method is a bit more complicated but results in beautiful work.

Additionally, when using an 8.5" × 11" page, you can print directly onto the layout page in creative forms and funky designs. Your pictures, stickers, and die-cuts can be placed on this page after text has been printed. With a little practice and some test prints, you can reposition your text and decide exactly where you want to print on the page.

For lettering, a term generally used for creating fun titles through an imaginative alphabet font, there are a number of CD-ROMs on the market that can assist you. Many come in themes such as weddings, children, school days, or holidays, but some on the market are general lettering programs with no specific subject in mind. Most allow you to print out the letters for use in the scrapbook, while others are tools that assist you in creating the lettering yourself. Either way, these are easy-to-use programs and you will no doubt be happy with the results.

**SSENTIALS**

It is a widely held belief that you should do your own lettering and journaling when scrapbooking. The biggest roadblock to this standard is that many people do not like their own handwriting. As much as you are encouraged to use your own print, nobody can force you to do anything!

Crafting with Clip Art

Clip art is computer generated imagery that can be placed in a scrapbook to help design a layout page. Originally published in book form, the term "clip art" came about because the art was make to be clipped out of these books with straight-edged scissors. These images can also be traced onto your acid-free paper by using a light-box or photocopied to allow opportunity for enlargement.

There are hundreds of Web sites that allow you to download free clip art. They usually have instructions on the site, and the images are very creative. If you have the means, this is a great alternative to buying clip art books or CD-ROMs. Once the clip art is downloaded, it can be sized to your needs and printed directly on acid-free paper. This can be clipped, or with 8.5" × 11" albums, the clip art can be printed directly on the layout page.

CHAPTER 6
Photography 101

At the heart of scrapbooking and memory books are pictures. They give us the ideas for our layouts. They are the pinnacle tools for our collections and our most cherished items. Photography is an art, and adhering to some simple standards can help your pictures truly capture your memories.

Photo Essentials

With the ease of point-and-click designs, we often forget just how many parts of the camera are essential in producing a good quality picture. Understanding the basic parts will help you to naturally increase your photographic skill level. There are hundreds of terms associated with photography, and if you pursue this as a hobby it is important to understand all of them. For our needs, however, the basic terms can help us begin to understand the art of photography.

FACTS

The word *photography* is derived from Greek meaning "light writing."

Aperture: The opening of a camera lens that allows light to enter.
Exposure: A combination of aperture size and shutter speed, allowing light to reach film.
Flash: A rapid burst of light.
Lens: Curved glass in the front of the camera that transfers light to film.
Shutter speed: The length of time the shutter remains open.
Viewfinder: An opening in the camera allowing the photographer to examine the subject.

A Crash Course in Cameras

Trying to purchase a camera without some knowledge of what is on the market is an arduous experience. Cameras can be expensive, and different styles will suit your different needs. For example, a point-and-shoot camera may be better if you intend to carry it with you at all times, while a disposable camera could be a better choice for vacations.

Point-and-Shoot Cameras

Little explanation needs to be made for point-and-shoot cameras. They are the most popular design of camera due to the ease and quality of the photos they produce. All varieties of this style of camera have the same concept: smooth operation and little need to adjust any settings. Among point-and-shoot cameras, however, there are a few that use a much higher level of technology. This is often reflected in both the quality of the pictures and the cost.

The most rudimentary point-and-shoot cameras have a flash that you turn on as needed. There are no other features included in the system. More advanced styles have buttons that allow you to zoom in and out, note the darkness, reduce red-eye, and switch to panoramic. Some are so well-developed that they do not allow a picture to be taken that is not in focus. If you have the money, these are wonderful alternatives to a basic point-and-shoot camera.

Disposable Cameras

Lightweight and easily transportable, disposable cameras are an invaluable tool for scrapbooking enthusiasts. While many people who are photography aficionados take care and pride in their style of camera and knowledge of photography, no one can argue the ease of the disposable.

Disposable cameras allow you to always have a camera on hand for the most unexpected picture moment. They are small and can easily be placed in a pocket, purse, diaper bag, or backpack without taking up too much room.

The quality of the disposable camera is good as well. While not ideal for a seasoned photographer, it is fine for an ordinary person trying to capture a fun moment. These cameras are especially good for children who are learning the basics of photography.

Instant Cameras

Some of the most fun cameras to use are instant cameras. Also known by the brand name Polaroid, these cameras are the ultimate in simplicity. The basic directions include pointing, clicking, and pulling the picture from the front. Children love to play with instant cameras. They are always a hit at birthday parties.

The drawbacks to instant cameras are abundant. They are not best for everyday use. The specialized film can be costly, and the system does not allow for negatives, making instant photos very difficult (but not impossible) to reproduce. More important, however, is that the pictures themselves are not the best quality. They tend to be smaller and can sometimes be out of focus.

Do not crop instant camera pictures! It will ruin a one-of-a-kind photo.

Single-Lens Reflex Cameras

Those of us who are not interested in pursuing photography as a hobby will probably never use a single-lens reflex (SLR) camera. These cameras are popular among amateur photographers because they allow for simplicity while also giving the photographer a large command over the camera.

SLR cameras permit you to change the shutter speed to truly capture the moment. The faster speeds allow for more precision and are used in action shots, while the slower speeds are adjusted to take more inactive photos. These cameras also include the ability to change the aperture settings, which will help adjust the brightness and focus of the photo. For example, you can adjust your camera to capture your child with a blurred background, or change the setting to focus on the pile of stuffed animals that surrounds him.

Digital Cameras

The technology to take photographs with a digital camera has become increasingly better throughout the years and continues to improve. While there are many similarities between digital and traditional cameras, particularly the general feel of the equipment, a digital camera is missing one important feature: film. To replace this is a mechanism called an image sensor that is comprised of pixels.

Digital photography is a great new tool for scrapbookers. It allows for fun elements to be added to pictures before placing them into the scrapbook. The purchase of a digital camera will most likely include photo-editing software. These programs allow you to do simple changes like crop a photo, add brightness, or soften the print.

FACTS

Pixels are tiny squares of images that make up a digital photograph. Similar to an impressionistic painting, one pixel contains no specific image, but added to millions of other pixels they capture and display the picture.

Additionally, it can help you to completely change the photo such as take unwanted elements out, change a picture from color to black-and-white, or add text. Become familiar with your editing program and try these fun elements, but be sure to save the original just in case you do not like the results.

Film

Film is the very heart and basic necessity of your pictures. It is important to take it seriously. Most brand names produce quality film, and all have expiration dates that reflect the film's freshness. Because film can be quite expensive, buying it in bulk is often a money-saving suggestion.

Film speeds are very simple to understand, but often are not recognized as an important feature for the camera. The film speed helps determine how the camera reacts to light. It is therefore very influential on the outcome of your pictures. To appreciate film speeds, get to know the characteristics of common speeds.

- **Slow Film**
  25 to 50 speed.
  Outdoor use only.
  Produces rich color, but high probability of unsharp images.
- **Medium Film**
  100 to 200 speed.
  Outdoor and some indoor use.
  Produces sharp images.

- **Fast Film**
  400 to 3200 speed.
  Outdoor and indoor use.
  Good in dim lighting and for capturing action photos.

Photo Composition

How many times have you taken a picture expecting wonderful results, only to come back from the processing center with something looking like it was taken by a four-year-old? Sometimes we are so engrossed in the moment and eager to snap a photo that we can forget some simple rules of picture composition.

 **ESSENTIALS**

Photo composition is also a great way to add variety to scrapbook pages. Think ahead about the layout and take photos at different angles. Snap the picture both side-to-side and up-and-down. Use the zoom lens for a close shot, and then step back to allow a lot of room around the subject. Use all angles in your layout for diversity in displaying the subject.

The first step is to ask, "What is your subject?" Use the viewfinder to help you decide what subject you want to focus on. Is your focus the child in front of the play gym, or the child with the play gym? The puppy sleeping, or the toys surrounding him?

Once you decide on the core figure of the picture, pay some attention to the details. The size of the object should enable it to be the main focus of the print, and subject matter around the focal point should complement it. How is the subject framed? What is the background, and how can this enhance the theme?

There is a rule in photography called "the rule of threes." This is important to understand for producing a skilled photo. It is as simple as breaking your photo into three equal parts and placing the subject into one of these sections.

Picture composition in thirds

Light the Way

Light is one of the most important elements of photography. Both the kind and direction of light should be taken into consideration when snapping a photo. How many times have you asked someone to stand in front of a window for a picture because the sunlight coming through looked so beautiful? Undoubtedly the picture did not turn out how you expected, and the subject was lost by the wrong use of lighting.

Natural light is comprised of moonlight and sunlight. The time of day, angle of the sun, or strength of the moon can all play a part in the outcome of the picture. Artificial light is common in light bulbs and flash photography. These types of light are interchangeable, as natural light can be used inside through doors, windows, or skylights, and flash photography is great to use outside in the shade or to complement the moonlight.

The direction of the light source can have important bearing on the subject matter. Frontlighting is best to show distinct parts of the subject. It is used when the source of light is to be behind the photographer.

This style of lighting is most popular; however, it allows for little depth to be shown in the subject.

SSENTIALS To avoid placing your shadow in a picture, consider moving both yourself and your subject into the shade. This will prevent any concerns about shadow placement, squinting, or sun spots and will still provide enough light to make a terrific picture.

Backlighting, when the light source is found behind the subject, produces a halo or silhouette effect. Other styles of light angles include sidelighting, a photographer's favorite, producing an uneven effect to illustrate objects, and overhead lighting, providing severe shadows and dramatic contracts.

Smile, You're on Candid Camera!

Candid pictures capture a natural atmosphere

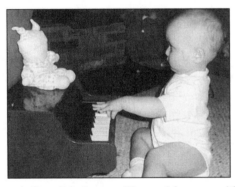

Both children and adults tend to immediately freeze up when they see a camera pointed at them. An attractive but nervous smile is flashed for the camera, and they often count the seconds until the picture is snapped. These photos are valuable, but do not catch the essence or mood of the situation.

Candid shots will provide you with the most natural and spontaneous pictures. They help depict an expression, an action, and a true feeling. Unstructured photos can show a shy infant, a gregarious toddler, a self-conscious teen, a tender moment, or a milestone. Even though we habitually pose for photographs, the candid shots are the pictures we cherish most.

The best way to take candid shots is to quietly have your camera handy. Let an activity be uninterrupted by your fiddling around, loading the film, or getting the subject in focus. Stay as far away as possible, and use your telephoto to get closer details. If at all possible, turn off the flash and have some noise in the background to drown out the camera buzz.

For candid shots of both children and adults, wait for a time when the subject is engrossed in an activity. Allow your child to play with a doll, have fun with the dog, or run around the outdoors without your interference. Tiptoe towards a father reading to his daughter or a son sticking his hand in a fishbowl. Deep concentration by your subject in an engaging activity is the best scenario in which to snap your photo.

FACTS

One of the best-known candid shots in American history was taken on February 19, 1945, at Iwo Jima, a tiny island in the South Pacific. After fighting and winning a long, hard battle with the Japanese, a small group of marines raised the American flag on top of Mt. Suribachi. This candid shot became a classic image of American triumph.

Black-and-White Photography

Black-and-white photography has enjoyed a resurgence in recent years. Once snubbed for color photographs, black and white prints are now hip and chic. Though popular for wedding photos, black-and-white pictures are also used to take candid shots of children, scenic images, and portraits.

FACTS

According to amateur photographer Eric Jarrell, point-and-shoot cameras are not optimal with black-and-white film. The auto-balance of the camera, a feature allowing the camera to recognize the film speed and adjust the shutter given the available light, will maximize the gray, resulting in less interest. The only way around this is to make sure you have high levels of natural contrast (bright and dark areas) within the picture.

Film for black-and-white photos is becoming more popular in discount department stores, but finding it at these retail outlets it is not a sure thing. Your best bet is to visit your local specialty camera shop and choose from a variety of films. The speeds are similar to color film, with the most common being 100, 400, 1600, and 3200.

Many amateur photographers using an SLR camera find black-and-white film to be intriguing and enjoyable. The balances with shadows and angles can make for some interesting photographs. On the other hand, users of point-and-click cameras are sometimes disappointed with the outcome of black-and-white photos because the images can be blurred or not as crisp as they had anticipated. In either case, taking quality pictures with black-and-white film takes practice. It is important to keep trying.

Tips of the Trade

Chances are that you already have enough photographs to fill several scrapbooks. It is for new pictures of family, friends, milestones, or other events that these tips will come in handy. To ensure you get pictures at some unforeseeable but memory-making times, take your camera with you and be ready to aim and shoot!

Children Make the World Go 'Round

Children are among the most popular picture subjects. They are easy to shoot in a playful and candid environment. They are naturally spontaneous. Chronicling their growth can be fun and an inspiration for scrapbookers.

For children, the closer the camera shot, the better the outcome. Capturing their expressions, joy, laughter, or deep concentration makes for a priceless photo. Telephoto lenses are especially good, allowing you to remain far enough away for anonymity while still securing the moment. The "rule of threes" is especially important with children's pictures. Avert your desire to automatically put the child in the center of the picture. Shoot it from one side or the other to depict his or her environment.

Our Best Friends: Pets

Family pets are among the most popular nonhuman photo subjects. They are so beloved that owners frequently try to capture these animals during fun-loving moments. More often than not, however, the pictures do not quite develop as we expect. Animal personalities are easy to get to know when you live with an animal, but these expressions are difficult to capture on film.

**SSENTIALS** Bring the camera down to the height of the animal when photographing your pet. This will allow you to get a natural angle instead of an awkward view from above.

When photographing your pet, try to use the outdoors as much as possible to avoid red-eye. High-speed film works best with action shots. If your pet quickly runs off, this film can capture the moment. Use pet favorites such as treats or toys, and avoid the midday hours. If you are very brave, try to take candid shots of child-pet interaction. It may take a few rolls of film, but chances are you will be pleasantly surprised with at least one or two pictures.

Milestones and Moments

Capturing significant moments in your life is a scrapbooking favorite. From a child's birth or first steps, to your graduation or wedding day, remembering these events through pictures is important.

Some of your bigger lifetime events may be put into the hands of a professional photographer. Other events, however, need to be captured for memories and family history. To capture milestones, try to tell the story with the photo. Remind yourself that many who will view the picture may not have been at the event to witness it, so be sure to capture as many elements and details into the print. Within your pictures, the following elements should be captured to truly preserve the memory of the day:

- Weather
- Setting
- Time
- Attendants

- Tangible elements (such as the mortarboard for a graduation shot, wedding cake)
- Facial expressions
- Candid shots

FACTS

The half-hours immediately after sunrise and immediately before sunset are known as the "Golden Hour." Using the right angles, they will provide a beautiful golden hue in your pictures.

Capturing Vacation Memories

Sometimes we are so caught up in experiencing a vacation, we forget to take pictures of the most memorable parts of the trip. Do you really need a roll of film of the touristy attractions of your trip? Is that where you received the greatest pleasure? Chances are you will talk more about your accommodations, restaurants, and other seemingly minute details when you get home. Capture these on film for your scrapbook—they allow you to truly relive the experience.

CHAPTER 7

Finding Creativity

By now you have organized your pictures, purchased needed tools, and found a place in your home to devote to scrapbooking. You are ready and eager to start—but all you can see is a stark white album page staring back at you. Where do you begin?

Creating a Theme

The most obvious place to start is with the memorabilia that you have already collected. Use color and designs that are specifically taken from these items. The background, weather, or actual event can sometimes be overlooked, when in reality they are the most obvious forms of inspiration. Pictures and souvenirs are the first step in creating the theme of your scrapbook page.

A Picture Says a Thousand Words

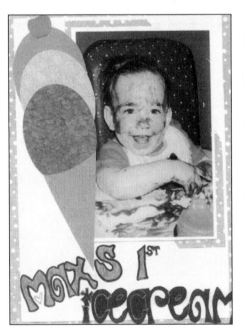

Scrapbook page for baby's first food

True, pictures most clearly tell the story, but a thousand words? Probably not. Through scrapbooking, however, you can truly retell the memory by complementing the picture with color, journaling, die-cuts, or other materials that contribute towards the account of the day. Use the picture to begin the story and the scrapbooking page will tell the rest.

For example, between four and six months of age, babies are often given their first taste of solid food. Pictures of this event are common, frequently capturing funny moments with a baby's face covered in food. These pictures tell half the story, and visually they are fun to have as a childhood milestone. The most important details however, particularly that it is the child's first meal of solid food, are left out.

Stimulating Souvenirs

Memorabilia that are specific to the event can also be a big inspiration. The colors of the memento, design of printed material, and event at which the keepsake was received should all be factors into designing your page. Layouts using wedding program souvenirs can be accented with bells or other wedding symbols for decoration. Colors can parallel those used for wedding itself (flowers, dresses, and so on).

When using any souvenirs in your scrapbook, it is important to buffer the item using a deacidification spray to prevent destructive materials, including acid, from migrating to other areas of the page.

Concert tickets, for example, have colors and lines printed that can help to identify some themes for your page. Use the ticket to begin telling the story and take bold elements from the ticket to design the items surrounding the memento. Figures such as musical notes, instruments, or other pieces that are specific to the performance can be included to add depth to the page. For devoted fans, take a picture to depict your enthusiasm such as waiting hours in a ticket line or of your musical collection.

The Good Old Days

Oral history was once one of the best ways to learn about the past. Talking with grandparents, great-grandparents, or other individuals that have lived a long life will not only be educational but enjoyable too.

A verbal account of history is also a great inspiration for your scrapbooking page. New and old photos brought together can result in some of your nicest pages. Expand your creativity into thinking outside the box, and allow the conversations with some older family members to be the stimulation for your scrapbook page.

Collecting this data now will allow future generations to share the memories too. After all, who but your great-grandmother truly remembers the weather on her wedding day? She's the only one who can give you specific details—perhaps she was late for the ceremony, the flowers were wrong, or maybe her dress was held up with a safety pin! She may now be comfortable and excited to reveal details that were once a secret, such as second thoughts or embarrassing bridesmaid incidents.

You may even discover hobbies of your older relatives and learn that they parallel those of you or your children. This might be a great time to capture some pictures of each of them performing their interests for your scrapbook page. Maybe your grandfather moonlighted as a boxer, or a great-grandfather was a volunteer fireman. Use this knowledge to create family history for your grandchildren and their grandchildren.

QUESTIONS?

What is scrapper's block?
Scrapper's block is a term used when you are creatively stalled in producing your layout pages. A common occurrence, most scrapbookers use many of the tips in this chapter to assist in sparking some ideas. The concept of scrapper's block is similar to writer's block, a phenomenon that authors often experience.

Additionally, speaking with the head of the family may reveal some things that were once not spoken. For example, you might find out that a great-grandparent was a bootlegger during Prohibition. This might have been kept hush-hush at the time, but it is a part of your family's history that can be passed along. In cases like this, find past newspaper articles to create the theme for the page along with a picture of your relative to truly preserve the memory.

Ask Questions

We often need a small nudge to jog our memories, particularly if you are poring over older pictures and trying to recall the details. Sometimes inspiration can come to us by simply asking some basic questions of either yourself or the subject. The answers to these questions might spark an idea or mold your creativity to creating the layout page.

- Who is in the picture?
- Who took the picture?
- What was the event or situation?
- Where was the picture taken?

- When was the event or situation?
- Why did the event or situation take place?

It is important to start with the picture itself to ask these basic questions. For example, for a picture whose subject is a group of people, asking the fundamental questions might reveal that they are all housemates in college. This may inspire a layout that includes a house or sketch of the dwelling to be the theme of the scrapbooking page.

Once the basic questions are answered, take a moment to respond to more specific inquiries about the day or event. The combination of answers will hopefully inspire you in your design.

- Who else was in attendance?
- What time of day did the event/situation take place?
- What was the specific setting?
- What did the event mean to you?
- What was the weather?
- Name funny moments.
- Name touching moments.
- Describe items involved (such as the birthday cake).
- Describe the event as a whole.

Kids Say the Dandiest Things

Sometimes the best sources of inspiration are our children. Their innocence allows for thinking that is not complex or spoiled by the environment. Their thoughts are natural, honest, and simple—the best elements for a scrapbooking memory.

Getting information from children can be difficult, but pointed questions help them to think clearly and understand the importance of details. This is not only beneficial for scrapbooking, it also makes a good exercise in using memory and recalling information. When asking questions of children, be sure to use a relaxed environment such as mealtime or after a nap. Trying to get information out of a hungry or sleepy child will no doubt be a challenging experience.

- Did you like the event?
- What do you remember about it most?
- What colors do you remember?
- What was your favorite part?
- Who did you talk with?
- Did anybody say anything funny?
- Do you want to do it again? Why?

Children particularly have a sense of simplicity that we should always revisit while scrapbooking. We can often get so caught up in the newest tools or technique that it is important to remember this concept. For example, you may be struggling for ideas to illustrate pictures from a community carnival because there is so much detail in the prints. Do you focus on the Ferris wheel, the roller coaster, or the cotton candy? Should you highlight the clown or the moon-bounce? Chances are, however, if you ask your son or daughter what they like most about the busy day, they will say something uncomplicated such as "I liked the red balloon." Voila! With this you realize that the ease of a background using a red balloon has inspired your page and will tone down busy prints.

Internet Forum Inspiration

Web forums bring together a group of people whose purpose is to find friendship in a craft that they all enjoy. Forums are one of the best places to get some inspiration. Message boards devoted to scrapbooking are all over the Internet. Finding them is easy, but determining which one is right for you will take a little time and patience. They are generally similar, allowing you to post comments, ideas, or questions, and requiring you to wait for the group to respond.

Scrapbooking communities on the Internet also have times set aside for chat room discussions. They usually have these posted on the board itself with a link to get to the site hosting the chat. These dedicated chats are wonderful for getting quick answers to your questions and boosting your sense of creativity. Asking a question such as "I would like to do a page of my daughter on the school bus, any ideas?" in the chat room will undoubtedly result in several suggestions for your design.

Be careful with divulging personal information when you join message boards or discussion forums. The Internet can be dangerous if you allow yourself to be too exposed. Consider using an alias when filling out basic information and creating a member name.

Independent Scrapbooking Stores

Independent or family-run scrapbooking stores are reminders of old-fashioned values in corner mom-and-pop shops. Everyone knows your name, and a smile always greets you at the door. It's not money-hungry businesspeople who have started these stores; instead, they're owned and operated by scrapbooking enthusiasts like yourself, who have discovered that they can make a living while doing something that they love.

Finding your creativity in an independent scrapbooking store can happen a few different ways. As with most stores, simply walking though and looking at different papers, tools, and writing utensils will inspire layout pages. These stores often have sample designs completed by the storeowner or workers to example some of the supplies offered. Smaller stores will frequently possess exclusive die-cuts or personal artwork that can be used for scrapbook pages—a luxury that the bigger chain stores or direct sales companies do not need to provide.

Still suffering from scrapper's block? Try organizing your supplies! Sorting tools and materials can inspire your imagination, and cleaning your workspace might help you to rediscover fun items you purchased months earlier.

Inspiration can also come from the store owner or workers. Unlike craft superstore chains, you will get personal service from expert scrapbookers. They will assist you in selecting your materials, offer tips on using tools, and give suggestions from their long history with the craft. Store owners and workers so love the art of scrapbooking that they are committed to lending a helping hand.

Additionally, "The Independents" (as they are known within the scrapbooking industry) offer personalized classes assisting in beginning the craft, targeting a subject, or perfecting a technique. Even the most experienced scrapbookers often attend classes when they feel that their creative juices are in a lull.

Other events sponsored by independent stores are crops and getaway weekends. The idea is to gather scrapbooking enthusiasts to have company while they work on their albums. Crops usually require a minimal fee, but this cost often goes towards food and drink. While there, you will have the opportunity to use tools and gather ideas that might not have come to you as quickly were you cropping alone.

Store-sponsored getaway weekends are becoming more and more popular. Usually held at a local hotel, they offer personalized classes, access to tools, food, mini-contests, door prizes, and overnight accommodations. Some organizations have even combined this with a spa weekend, allowing time to crop and time to be pampered by experts at a luxury facility. These often sell out months in advance.

Magazines, Web Sites, and Books

The amount of resources for scrapbookers is tremendous. Sifting though all of these materials can be confusing. What information can you trust? Who has your best interests at heart?

As a general rule, all magazines, Web sites, and books provide dependable information. Some may describe techniques better than others may, but overall most can help. More than anything else, resources such as these can give you design ideas and spark your imagination. Use them when you are stuck on a page or need a boost, or when you're just looking for new ideas.

Web Site Wonderland

The Internet not only provides scrapbookers with friendships through message boards, it also brings us hundreds of Web sites devoted to our craft. If you explore the Internet through a search engine using the keyword *scrapbooking*, chances are your results will reach into the thousands.

The most elaborate sites out there, and undoubtedly the ones that try to get to you first, are virtual scrapbooking retail stores. Most sites are good, and if you want to buy tools or materials, many of them will have better deals than local scrapbooking stores. Some retail stores will also provide articles on trendy techniques or current scrapbooking events. Many of these are good resources and can help spark your creativity. Keep in mind, however, that their ultimate goal is to make money, and ulterior motives can be possible.

The sites that are brought to you as a Web magazine are ideal for scrapper's block. They are informative and provide quality information. Most have departments as with any paper magazine, as well as daily, weekly, and monthly features. The great thing about Web magazines is that you can sort through archived articles and features, so tips and suggestions are always at your fingertips. Additionally, Web magazines have archived hundreds of sample layouts. Use these to inspire your pages, but as always, be sure to include some original creativity in the finished product.

SSENTIALS Sometimes a break from scrapbooking can be just the right situation to cure scrapper's block. Walk away for a few days, put everything aside, and forget about layouts and pictures. Chances are when you return you will feel rejuvenated and motivated.

Some of the best sites are personal scrapbooker's pages. They do not try to sell you items and generally do not ask you to visit their sponsors. Personal Web sites are simply provided by scrapbookers who want to share their pages. Their reasons for creating pages are varied. Many want to share to show off their children. Others are especially proud to exhibit a special layout. Additionally, personal scrapbookers offer trade tips, individual suggestions, or ideas that have brought them success.

Print Magazines

Print magazines are easy to pick up for some inspiration if you are in a bind. They are fun to read and always have beautiful pages. As with any periodical, specialty scrapbooking magazines have feature articles that detail fun ideas and difficult techniques. The magazines also have departments featuring different tools, lettering, tips, and other categories each month.

Print magazines are inexpensive if you subscribe to an annual home delivery, but purchased from the newsstand they can cost up to $5 each. The money is usually worth it, as you will no doubt find some inspiration in the pages. It has been said, however, that scrapbookers sometimes feel intimidated by the high quality of the layout pages. Use these magazines to stimulate an idea for your album, but do not let expert artwork cause any stress. Always remember that there are no wrong scrapbooking pages.

Book Haven

As you have probably noticed, this is not the only book on the shelves that can assist you with scrapbooking. There are a number of quality books that are dedicated to certain techniques and styles of layout pages. As with other tools, check out the book before you make your purchase. Read through it, and figure out if the description in the book is the same information you can get from free sources such as the Internet or an independent scrapbooking store.

Purchasing a book on lettering, for example, might be useful if all of your other ideas have been exhausted and you are excited to try something new. Before you go to the bookstore, however, look for lettering articles on the Internet or in print magazines—and of course, browse through the lettering section of this book. If you still want to purchase a specialty book after looking through these resources, sift through the table of contents and be sure that it is comprehensive and worth the money.

Inspirational Ideas

Using a cereal box for inspiration

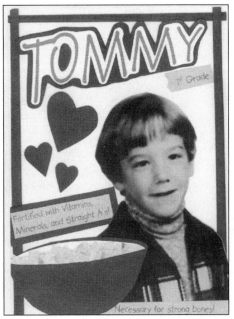

Colors and designs surround us through print and television media. Shopping centers flash us with glitzy advertisements and colorful shopping bags. Even paper towels, tissue boxes, and book covers have designs that would be beautiful page backgrounds. Ideas for scrapbooking pages surround us everyday, but they can be easily missed if you do not simply open your eyes to the possibilities.

Most of the ideas are simple. Still, they are often the inspiration that allows us to think creatively about our pages. Using a shopping bag, for example, you can copy or trace the design to reconfigure it for the background of your layout. It is important to remember that these are simply for ideas. Actually using the bag would allow acidic products onto the page. Using card stock, simulate the bag design onto your scrapbook page.

CHAPTER 8

Layout Principles

L ayouts reflect mood and atmosphere of the memory itself. Determining what kind of layout you produce will probably have a lot to do with the theme. Creating lively, romantic, or colorful layouts is where the questions of proper design arise. Some basic layout principles can assist in your decision-making process.

Composition

The composition of a layout page is at the heart of creating quality scrapbooking designs. Too often there is excessive focus placed on one detail and not enough on the overall look of the page. Perhaps this is due to too many pictures, too little journaling, no target theme, overuse of cropping, or a number of other common oversights.

FACTS

Graphic artists use five basic principles of design when developing a visual piece: balance (evening out the elements), contrast (incorporating diversity), harmony (creating unity in the elements), rhythm (establishing eye motion), and proportion (associating sizes and shapes).

Sometimes you do not even realize that your page composition is not solid until it is finished, and by then it may be too late. Some simple steps to creating scrapbooking layout composition will assist in the design of your page.

Central Point

All pages should have an agenda, also known as a focus. Figure out who or what element of your page deserved the most emphasis. Let the layout be determined through this theme. The theme should be clear by using decorative materials including die-cuts, clip art, descriptive lettering, and colors. These tools can help the focus gain momentum throughout the page.

Sometimes the theme can be completely predetermined and guided by your use of titles. For example, at first glance, a picture taken at a family picnic and a picture taken at a bridal shower should have little reason to be on the same scrapbooking page. This standard changes, however, if you choose to focus on the person in the pictures instead of on the events.

Tell a Story

The composition of a page heavily depends on the scrapbooker telling a story. While this idea automatically makes us think of journaling, telling the story is also a visual element with decoration and pictures. Randomly selecting photos with nondescript phrases or little meaning ignores some basic composition styles.

The use of color in your layout can have a strong impact on the person viewing the page. Use warm colors such as reds, oranges, and yellows to add the emotion of excitement, drama, and even danger. Cool colors, such as blues, purples, and greens, should be used to complement layouts portraying themes like tranquility and patience.

The composition, however, goes beyond just telling the basics of a central story line—telling it in sequence is just as important. For example, a page depicting a child's birthday party might have pictures of gifts, children, wrapping paper, and games. A page that first depicts presents being unwrapped or children eating cake and then shows children arriving does not truly show the order of the story. Page composition appears confusing if the story does not have some sort of sequence.

A Movement Mandate

The movement of the page is as important as the order of your story. Movement and order are essentially intertwined with one another. You use movement, or the flow of the page, to move the reader's eye across the layout in the direction you desire.

You can control movement by using strategically placed stickers, die-cuts, or lettering. Movement also has a lot to do with the angle of your pictures or the design in which they were cropped. Some common uses of depicting movement include simple or decorative dashes, weather (lightning, clouds, snowflakes, rain), and animals moving from picture to picture.

What is symmetry?
According to the dictionary, symmetry is the correspondence of opposite parts in size, shape, and position, resulting in a measure of balance or beauty.

The Balance Beam

Creating balance within a scrapbook page

Balancing your page takes a little familiarity with the ideas of composition, but for the most part anyone with a good eye can tell when a page is not symmetrical. It generally means that your design should be spread evenly throughout the page and not concentrated in one area. This does not mean that you should have a picture in each of the page's four corners, but it does mean that it's important to balance both sides of a design with some material to level the eye.

Balance is an integral part of each page, as well as the overall look of the scrapbooking layout. This is particularly important in journaling for the layout. Instead of writing above a picture to depict its events, place the text off-center. To balance this section of the page, create a design or use a die-cut on or below the picture on the opposite side.

Shapes and Patterns

Using shapes and patterns in your layout can easily turn a run-of-the-mill memory book to a work of art. Using them together or separately can complement pictures, lettering, journaling, and other essential scrapbooking materials. They add texture, design, and they also help maintain a theme in the page. Patterns often assist the momentum of the page and give the layout some depth.

Shape Up!

The standard shapes are circles, squares, and triangles. Other common shapes used in scrapbooks include hearts, stars, puzzle pieces, diamonds, and numerous geometric shapes. Shapes can have enough emphasis to help create the theme, or they can be minimized to simply complement it. Consider using a shape when selecting a title. You can also use a shape for journaling or add it to backgrounds as a design supplement.

FACTS

Shapes have psychological associations, and using them in your scrapbook pages can create certain feelings in those who view the page. Circles represent infinity and the feeling of protection. Triangles give the feeling of conflict or action being taken. Squares represent equality and truthfulness.

Patterns in Paper

Patterned paper is popular for both complementing a page and emphasizing a focal point. Patterns come in all shapes and sizes. In addition to being used for backgrounds, they can be cut and used in journaling, matting pictures, punch art, borders, page breaks, and other decorative means.

Some of the designs on patterned paper are very specific. You might use paper designed with dog bones for your "New Puppy" page, or a safari-textured page to show your trip to the zoo. Winter holiday paper is often adorned with evergreen trees, religious symbols, holly, candles, and snow. Seasonal paper is usually found in the colors and objects that represent that time of year. The paper can be designed with décor on its borders only, or it can be spread evenly on the page.

Other patterned papers offer designs that are not so specific for your layout. These usually have a simple pattern added to one base color. These styles are a great alternative to some of the more dramatic patterns offered. You might find that a simple pattern on a pink base is just right for a baby-girl page instead of a more highly patterned design with bottles and pacifiers.

Creating Patterns

Patterns are not limited to prefabricated paper. They can be created freehand with shapes and contrasts or by using a template, punch, or other cutting system to help create the design. These are fun to help with borders, page breaks, or to adorn the edge of pictures or die-cuts.

It is important not to crop one-of-a-kind photos that do not have negatives! Consider instead placing a frame mat over the picture to ensure that no elements are lost. If you are determined to crop the picture, make a color photocopy and crop this first to determine that you are making the correct decision for your layout.

Punches, smaller die-cuts, and even stickers are often used to create a pattern. So is paper cut into particular shapes. Dolls cut to form a chain are a common pattern, as are elements that reflect the theme of a particular layout. A set of snowflakes placed one after another creates a pattern across a winter wonderland page, or nonspecific patterns like squiggles can simply be placed together to create an artistic element.

Contrast

Have you ever seen a room decorated with a floral sofa and striped pillows? If the colors are based in the same family or cut from the same material, it might give your room a little character and texture. Now, picture the same room but add a striped rug, floral curtains, floral lampshades, and textured wall paper . . . suddenly your contrasts have gone too far.

The same can be said for scrapbooking pages. Some contrast is beneficial and can help the pages look less static. It is easy, however, to use too much contrast and make the page far too busy. You can quickly get lost in a fun technique or attractive paper and allow the page to be too difficult on the eye.

Shapes are so common in scrapbooking that they are often overlooked as an element where contrast can be achieved. Use them in opposition to draw attention to the focal point of the page. Apply two straight lines to border a circle, or a floral pattern as a background to a triangle. A square picture that you do not want to crop can be surrounded by different patterned or colored shapes, or mounted on a collage of circles.

Color is a good tool for creating contrast in your design. For example, black backgrounds with white writing can stand out more than using less distinct colors. The dominant color in a picture can be contrasted with a different color backing, or a plain color can be added to the mounting materials of patterned paper. Sometimes contrasts in picture backing will allow the picture to stand out more. Contrast can also be used the other way to tone down a busy print.

The contrast in your layout will often catapult it from dull to dynamic in an instant. Allow the contrast to be interesting instead of monotonous, and do not be afraid to try something new.

Picture Matting

Your layout will no doubt contain pictures. The way you mat them can make all the difference in your scrapbooks. You can tone down busy prints, liven up the dull ones, or complement the subject by making the right decisions in your matting materials and style. Pictures can be placed either above the mat paper or below to create a framed look.

Bright red might look great on one person but look terrible on another. The same can be said for picture matting. Colors bring out different elements in pictures, and the mat paper used in your layout will have a direct effect on how the photo appears.

Matting will help to create your layout by adding shapes—a key factor in the final design outcome. While the shape of the mat often reflects the shape in which the photo has been cropped, the layout element of contrast is an important factor in your matting decision. For example, you might crop a photo into a circle, then mat it onto a square backing. Other contrasts include using a light backing on a dark photo or a bright background on a muted print. Some of the most distinct background mats come from using mats in the red family with black and white prints.

Patterned paper is probably the most popular material for matting photos. With hundreds of styles to choose from, you can find patterns ranging from elegant wedding mats to lively birthday party themes. Some trendy mat materials include vellum and mulberry paper. Vellum, a translucent paper, is wonderful for creating a classic and chic look. Mulberry can be used to create a wispy mat and a poetic finish.

Layout Templates

The more you hone your skills in scrapbooking, the more comfortable you will feel creating your own layouts. It won't take long before you get an instinctive knack for the rules of artistic composition and design. Until you reach that point, it is important to keep trying. Eventually it will be fun to look at early pages and compare them to the pages you are doing after you've gotten some practice.

FACTS

Some layout templates are designed papers onto which you simply adhere cropped pictures in designated areas of the page. Other layout templates act as a model instead of a physical page, and still others simply guide you in copying your idea.

There are times in the beginning that you might need some inspiration producing layout pages. Templates are a good answer. They can save you time and also get you moving on to the next page more quickly.

Prefabricated Layouts

Prefabricated layout paper often comes in theme packs at the craft store. It is already full of color and design. All you need to do is to crop the pictures you want on the page and place them into the designated areas.

Prefabricated pages can be helpful, but using them excessively requires very little imagination on your part. The pages might not quite reflect the mood of the event or idea you are trying to express. Instead of using the entire page, some scrappers cut the template and use a portion of the design to complement their layout. This is a good alternative. It allows you to be a little more creative while still saving you some time.

Stencil Layouts

Layout stencils allow you to trace a design onto an album page and then use your own colors, paper, and pictures to adorn the page. Most stencil include a few places for pictures and a section to journal. Once you pencil the design onto your scrapbook page, there is no reason why it cannot be decorated with papers, stickers, or die-cuts. The stencil simply allows you to strategically place the major elements, but the end result is up to you.

Layout stencil

Scrapbook
page using
layout stencil

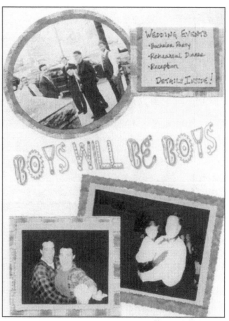

The first figure shows a sample stencil template. Stencils are usually made from a hard plastic sheet, with holes cut to allow your writing instrument to easily trace the layout. Each hole represents an area for you to trace onto the page. Once the layout template is fully traced, use patterned paper for mats in the photo and journaling areas. Place your pictures. Look at the design and decide if you can use any additional elements, such as die-cuts or stickers. It is amazing how a little color can spruce up a stencil template!

Now look at the layout again once it's complete. While still using the basic layout template design, a little decoration allowed the page to have some unique qualities and a personal touch.

ESSENTIALS

Although it is not recommended that the template be used on every album page, different patterns and colors will also permit you to use the same template on a few pages throughout the album without looking too monotonous. The stencil can also be flipped to create a flowing two-page spread.

Borrowing Layouts

When you design your pages, there is nothing wrong with borrowing layouts from other sources such as this book, magazines, or Web sites. Sure, scrapbooking stresses individual creativity and ideas, but there's nothing wrong with taking a design from someone else every once in a while, especially if the layout fits your needs. Borrow layouts when you are stuck and need something to jump-start your artistic flow—in other words, save them for when you really need a jolt.

Several Web sites allow you to download layout templates that you can use in your album, and magazines have particular areas that they encourage you to copy straight out of the book. Remember, scrapbooking is subjective, and two layouts that have the same placement of elements can look extremely different in the end.

Less Is More

Some specialized page styles incorporate many different elements to capture a number of memories in one layout. Layout quilts and collages are probably the best examples of these specialized styles. While pages such as these depend on using many materials and pictures, the everyday scrapbooking layout does not need so many factors to creatively express your memory.

Scrapbook page using one photo

Most scrapbook pages have more than one picture per page, creating variety and enhancing the theme. While it might be difficult, it is important to use only good quality pictures in your scrapbook. Ask yourself if you really need five pictures of the same scene if you have two good shots that have really have captured the subject well.

Remember that you want your scrapbook to be appealing to everyone who sees. It might be more important to remove one picture and create some space for journaling than to include pictures that are out of focus or blurry. When surrounded by the right elements, one single photo per page can be just as dramatic a way to capture memories as an album full of photos.

The "less is more" concept also applies to the materials used in your layout. Try not to overuse patterned paper or fancy techniques that might overpower the memory you are trying to preserve. Using too many accessories on your layout page can diminish even the best intentions. Going overboard can derail an otherwise well designed page composition. On the flip side, too few accessories can make an arrangement look boring. Try to stay away from these common composition blunders:

- Too many photos/too few photos
- Too little color
- Color of different hues (such as deep winter colors with pastels)
- Using too many shapes
- Overcropping photos
- Misplaced journaling
- Too many stickers
- Too many die-cuts/clip-art

ESSENTIALS

Put aside the nonessential elements that you want to use for your scrapbook page (that is, the things you want to use to embellish your primary design elements, such as the photograph). Once the layout is almost complete, add these elements one by one until the layout is done. Adding all of these elements in the beginning might take up space you need for necessary page elements such as titles, journaling, or photographs.

The Two-Page Spread

Some times you will have five or six photos that you would like to use together in one layout. One scrapbook page doesn't give you space to include this many prints. By using a two-page spread, meaning the back of one album page and the front of the next, you can effectively use all six photos and only need one theme, one title, and so on. A two-page layout lends the scrapper a lot of creativity, flexibility, and space.

If you do use two pages for one layout, strongly consider design elements to ensure that both pages are brought together with the same style, colors, techniques, etc. The concept of movement in page design is particularly important in a two-page layout, as you will want the reader's eye to automatically flow from one page to the next without processing a break.

If you use the front and back of your album pages, pay close attention to your album binding when you have completed about thirty pages. The materials on each page can make the album heavy and less structurally sound. Consider starting a new album to hold more pages.

This is particularly important to consider—and difficult to achieve—with ring-bound albums where the middle rings often break up the page momentum. Book, strap-hinge, and post-bound albums are best for creating two-page layouts because the break between pages is minimal in these album styles.

Things to Keep in Mind

Practice makes perfect, and you will no doubt improve with basic layout principles as you continue to create scrapbooking pages. It is important to remember that the rules for standard layout design are the same for all the graphic arts. Adhering to these basic principles will get you on the right track. Once you understand focus, balance, contrast, and movement, a few more minor elements can help perfect your layout techniques:

- Keep room for journaling.
- Add stickers or die-cuts to vast spaces.
- Be comfortable with white space in layouts.
- Use fonts/lettering that reflect the layout.
- Be consistent throughout the page.
- Know the reason behind all your page layout decisions.
- Make the layout less uniform and static and more visually appealing.
- Make sure the end result is pleasing to the eye.

CHAPTER 9
Journaling Basics

As you organized your pictures, they probably brought you back a flood of old memories. Chances are, however, that you couldn't remember everything about all your pictures. Who are the people at this holiday party? Where did you take this camping trip? What year was this family reunion? In this chapter we'll discuss the concept of journaling, a proven technique for saving details of cherished memories.

Record Memories Now, Journal Later

Using layout elements to journal

Many details are lost over time. The reason we journal can be diminished if we wait so long enough that we forget some precious details in the meantime. Journaling immediately after the event can seem like a nuisance, particularly if you do not plan on scrapbooking the memory for some time.

If you consider that the experience itself has the same importance as the picture you're taking, that can sometimes help to put journaling—and its importance— into a new light. Jotting down notes to record the memory can in time become second nature, as natural as pointing the camera.

One of the easiest ways to get into the habit of immediately recording details of a memory is to keep a small journal with you at all times. Carry it in your purse or in your car. Use it only for journaling memories, writing down quotes, or keeping ideas for scrapbook pages. Buy a small enough notebook that it is not a bother to tote around.

Use acid-free paper if you store your memory cards with the pictures themselves. Index cards are ideal, but the are not guaranteed to be of archival quality. Cut acid-free paper into index card sizes to write down your memories.

There are hundreds of fancy journals on the market that you can use for this purpose, but this is an area where you do not need to be crafty! A simple note pad will suffice and only costs a few pennies at a local drug store or supermarket.

Most scrappers store pictures away until they are ready for use in the layout page. Important details are in the greatest danger of being lost from the time you take a picture until the time you pull it for use in your scrapbook. You can keep those details out of danger with a simple method. Use a small form as a memory record card to capture the memory immediately and use it as a journaling key at a later date. Once they're filled out, you can store your memory record cards with your pictures. This will help you to journal with rich detail well after the event has otherwise faded into the past.

Memory
Record Card

Memory Record Card

What is the memory?

Who was there?

Why did it occur?

Where did it occur?

When did it occur?

What was the season/weather?

How did you feel?

Most memorable moments:

Subtle observations:

Memorable quotes of the day:

Walking the Straight Line

A lot of scrapbookers get caught up in producing straight lines for their journaling. Straight lines are ideal and easy to read, but the process of making them does not have to be stressful! Straight lines are easy to make with a little help from both basic and inventive tools.

The most basic and least expensive way to create straight lines is to use a ruler and a light pencil. Draw the lines without pressing hard, and write over them with your journaling pen. Test to be sure the ink will not smear, and then erase the lines with a soft eraser. Be aware that pencil might show through some light inks such as white or yellow, so a soft touch with pencil lead is very important.

ESSENTIALS

On prelined paper used for journaling, cover unused black lines with stickers or die-cuts to prevent the lines from intruding into the layout of your page.

One of the most inventive new products is a pen whose ink disappears 48 hours after you write with it. You can use it in combination with a ruler to create lines for journaling. Since it needs no erasing, this pen also prevents the possibility of smearing your journaling ink.

You can also buy paper that is preprinted with straight lines. Lines come preprinted on all kinds of scrapbooking materials, including album pages, heavy card-stock, and some patterned paper. While the lines are sometimes light, they usually come in basic black. Preprinted lined paper is not an ideal tool as the lines often distract from your layout.

Block and Bullets

The standard form of journaling is to write each section in a paragraph form. The paragraphs usually appear as a block of text strategically placed somewhere on the layout. There are alternatives to laying out your journaling elements that can add a little variety to your album and a touch of creativity to each page.

The Top Ten List

In a style similar to David Letterman's famous "Top Ten List," arrange your details in order from number ten so that they move toward the number one detail you would like to remember. This top-ten list explains the details of the day and builds up to the most memorable moment.

For example:

Top Ten Memories for Our Neighborhood Halloween Party, 2000!

10. Beautiful weather prompted the entire community to join us.
9. Children were dressed as Hershey's Kisses, dragons, princesses, alligators, etc.
8. The park was dedicated and new playground-safe equipment was in place. All of the children loved the swings, slides, monkey bars, and playground tires.
7. Marie was put into a swing for the first time. She was a little scared, but we gently held her as we moved the swing back and forth. Eventually we got a smile!
6. The other children were all friendly to Marie, who was the youngest child at the party. They all wanted to come up to her and say hello.
5. All of the children received a bag of goodies for Halloween treats.
4. Marie joined the other children to march in a parade. Since they were lined up by age, Marie went first.
3. A three-judge panel for the costume contest included a township supervisor.
2. It was such an exciting day, Marie was so tired toward the end and started to fall asleep in Daddy's arms. So cute!

And the #1 memory of the Halloween Party . . .

1. Dressed as a lamb, Marie won First Place!

Bullet Lists

Using bullet lists can save you time. Usually reserved for short, choppy sentences, a bullet list provides little expression beyond the facts.
For example:

2000 Community Halloween Party

- Marie won first place in the costume contest!
- Clear and sunny skies.
- Costumes included Hershey's Kisses, dragons, princesses, and alligators.
- Park was dedicated and equipped with safe materials.
- Marie was put into the swing for the first time.
- Marie was the youngest to attend.
- Treats were given to children.
- Children marched in a parade by age, Marie went first.
- Marie started to fall asleep at the end.

On the Edge

Another style of journaling is to write around the outer edge of the picture mat. This usually calls for a small description, perfect if you just want to write a line or so about the subject. This is also an excellent technique for adding balance to a page, adding some depth to an otherwise static look, or fitting in a sentence where there are no blocks of space available.

ESSENTIALS

Using journaling to create movement in a page can be unconventional and add some pizzazz. Instead of creating one block of text, write each sentence in the same movement as the pictures, and include text at each point that you would like the reader's eye to focus.

Journaling Imagery

On the outside, journaling and images seem like two different elements of the scrapbook page. Your journal text, however, can promote your theme by combining it with images that the theme possesses. This style of journaling can help to creatively figure out just how you are going to fit the text onto the page. Think outside the norm and create a way to journal that brings your audience's eyes to the focus instead of away from it.

FACTS

Journaling Genie has a software program that allows you to easily combine text with images for creative, fun, and inventive styles on your layout page. They average $25 and can be found at many local scrapbooking stores or on the Internet.

Use bigger die-cuts for this form of journaling. Before you write on it, be sure you know exactly where the die-cut will fit into your layout. If your picture will cover some of the die-cut, take this into consideration when journaling onto the piece so that you leave some room for the picture.

Using
die-cuts
to journal

July 2001: MESA, AZ
We spent all day at the dude
Ranch. John loved the horses
and even sat on a pony! We
stayed through dinner and
a very tired baby
slept all the
way home. Looking
forward to
next year!

WANTED

Computer clip-art is fun to use for journaling. Cut and paste the clip-art into a word processing program where you can easily enlarge it to the size you desire for the scrapbook page. Create a text box within the image and eliminate the outside line. You can then use a rotation system to make it look as if it was designed to hold the text.

Use it also to create your layout instead of complement your layout. Any image can be changed to include journaling if you use just a little imagination! Write a sentence in lieu of a balloon string, create text in place of clock hands, or allow words to replace a flower stem.

Using Computers to Write Text

Personal handwriting is preferred in journaling, but computer-generated text does put a lot of variety almost effortlessly at your fingertips. A word processing program includes a diverse selection of fonts that can help with the mood of the layout. A script font might be appropriate for a romantic page, while a juvenile-looking font is better for a child's page.

Fonts can be easily downloaded from the Internet. Most sites offering free fonts clearly describe each step of the process. Free font sites will usually allow you to download the new fonts in a compressed, or "zipped," format. This means that your computer needs a decompression program such as WinZip. These are also widely available for free on the Internet.

You can also get variety in your journaling style by changing the angle of a block of text or by using a text art function in your word processing program. If you have a color printer, color text that corresponds with the page or shading or paintbrush functions will give you even more added variety.

Not Exactly My Own Words

Journaling does not end with telling your story in your own words. You can keep going by adding meaningful poems, related quotes, or song lyrics. Adding these elements can bring you back to the memory through the senses. A quote or poem will elegantly express how you feel about your family, friends, children, or spouse.

Finding meaningful written words can be easy if you know where to look. There are numerous books of famous quotations and meaningful poems, and the Internet is one of the easiest place to look for text. Web sites devoted to quotes, lyrics, and poems can be found with just a few keystrokes through any Internet search engine. Enter a search term such as "love poems," and the search engine will return a selection of Web sites devoted to love poems of all kinds.

It is important to give credit where credit is due! If using a quote, poem, or song lyric in your scrapbook, make sure you also write the author's name next to the text. Copyright issues may not seem significant in a personal scrapbook, but it's important to show the proper respect to the artists whose work adds so much meaning to your pages.

Song lyrics also have a big fan base on the Internet. If there's a song you constantly hum and you want to use it in your layout, you can look up the lyrics by simply typing the name of the song and the artist into a search engine along with the word *lyrics*. You will probably find a few sites that have the exact song lyrics written out for you.

And You Can Quote Me!

Quotes can be found by searching author, keyword, or subject. Try Web sites such as ✍ *www.famous-quotations.com* and others that are popular reference sites. Quotes can also be used to signify particular situations; they do not have to be general love, family, or friendship quotations. For example, if you have a picture of your son in a Halloween spacesuit costume, you might quote Obi Wan Kenobi, in *Star Wars*: "There is a great disturbance in the force." Other movie quotes, such as Robert De Niro's unforgettable "You talkin' to me?" from *Taxi Driver*, or Bogie's famous "Here's looking at you, kid" from *Casablanca* are also fun examples.

If you spend some time researching quotes, chances are you will come up with just the right one for your scrapbook page. Pictures of children are especially fun to caption with famous sayings, as many adult-oriented remarks make the scene even more amusing. For example, with a picture of your five-year-old posing in cool black shades, you might use the popular Blues Brothers quote, "It's 106 miles to Chicago. We got a full tank of gas, half a pack of cigarettes, it's dark and we're wearing sunglasses. Hit it!"

Poetry, Prose, and Personality

Poetry is the ultimate in expression using words. Creating poetry on your own is most thoughtful, and if you have the time and interest, it is a rewarding hobby. Borrowing poetry might not be as personal, but it is just as moving and can save you time. Poetry can be used on any page, and depending on the subject and length, can be a subtle addition or a bold focus. Verses on friendship, love, and family will add an emotional element.

The writings of Jane Austen, known best for their interesting take on the subject of love, contain some of the finest and funniest quotations pertaining to courtship and marriage. Peruse her novels to find a good line for scrapbook layouts about dating, engagements, or weddings.

There are a number of styles of poetry that you can use. One favorite of scrappers is called a name acronym. It take the letters of any name and makes each one into the beginning of a sentence. It might take a little while, but eventually the words will come to you. Make sure you have a picture of the person with you while writing the poem to help spark some memories and creativity.

Michele Niec wrote the following is a name acronym poem for John Charles:

Just like my dreams
Of a Prince
Holding my hand
No more sorrow . . . You came into my Life.

Carefully stepping
Heart open wide
As it should be
Rest with me
Lie by my side
Endless passages of love
Safe . . . You came into my Life.

Famous poetry is a popular way to make scrapbook pages more expressive. For example, chances are you know at least a few lines from this celebrated Elizabeth Barrett Browning sonnet:

How do I love thee? Let me count the ways.
I love thee to the depth and breadth and height
My soul can reach, when feeling out of sight
For the ends of Being and ideal Grace.
I love thee to the level of every day's
Most quiet need; by sun and candlelight.
I love thee freely, as men strive for Right;
I love thee purely, as they turn from Praise.
I love thee with the passion put to use
In my old griefs, and with my childhood's faith
I love thee with a love I seemed to lose
With my lost saints,—I love thee with the breath.
Smiles, tears, of all my life!—and, if God choose,
I shall but love thee better after death.

Journaling Creations

As important as journaling is to the process of capturing your memories in your scrapbooks, it can still be one of the most tedious parts of the process. No written rule says that you have to use any of the journaling styles mentioned in this chapter. Look within your memory and take ideas from the layout subject to help you come up with something completely fun and different for journaling. Ideas such as journaling books, newspaper clippings, recipes, or letters will creatively change the look of your page.

Journaling Book

Journaling book

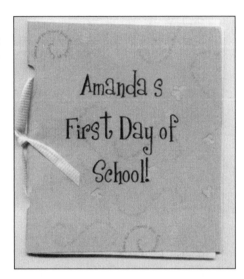

Creating a journaling book within your layout is easy and adds a three-dimensional element to your page. Simply fold two cut pieces of light acid-free card stock in half. Punch holes in the spine and thread through a thin piece of string to bind the book together. Create a book cover that complements the layout page, and journal on inside pages of the book. Once this is complete, use adhesive on the back of the book to attach it to the layout page.

Check your pens before journaling on one-of-a-kind scrapbooking materials! It is easy to pick up the wrong style of pen and begin to write, only to realize much too late that you accidentally picked up the brush pen instead of the fine point. Also make sure that your pens have not frayed or dried out before you use them on a die-cut.

Mom's Home Cooking

A recipe can be a fun way to show what went into the memory—and how it turned out in the end! It can be written on a recipe card that you have buffered or on a recipe card that you create on acid-free paper. Either way, the memory is expressed in a more interesting way than simply writing a block of text.

Using a
recipe card
to journal

From the kitchen of: Mommy & Daddy   Date: 9-5-2001
Recipe for: Amanda's 1st day of school

Ingredients:
1 Plaid gumper Dress & Saddle Shoes
1 Butterfly Nametag
2 Loving Parents
1 Teacher named Mrs. Burns
16 Classmates
1 Sunny day
2 Pencils, 1 Box of Crayons

© by Colorbök

Extra Extra!

Newspaper headlines are natural attention-grabbers. They are often used as creative ways to title a page. Instead of stopping with a newspaper headline, why not write your journaling piece in the style of a newspaper, too? You will probably come out with a fun "article" that makes the memory sound like it was written by a reporter on the scene. If you format your article in a word processing program and print it out on ivory paper, you'll create an authentic look in an especially creative way to use this style of journaling.

Amanda Sails Through First Day of School

PHILADELPHIA PA—The first day of school for Amanda was a sunny September day in 2001. She could barely sleep the night before and ran into Mom and Dad's room before the morning alarm could sound. Breakfast came early that morning, full of energy and protein for an exciting day ahead. After all of the eggs were finished and the dog was walked, Amanda put on her new plaid jumper and saddle shoes, grabbed her back-pack and quickly ran to the corner to await the school bus. She jumped onto it with gusto, and did not even care that her parents followed behind in their car. At school she met Mrs. Burns, her new teacher, and got to know 16 classmates. Amanda wore a butterfly nametag so that everyone would get to know her easily. Time went by fast, and Amanda was very anxious for nap hour to arrive. She came home with new friends and was eager to return the next day. We hope this happiness for education lasts another twelve years!!

Letters from the Heart

Writing a letter on the scrapbook page can add a sentimental and personal touch to journaling. Write in a style that allows the letter to be expressed "from me to you." The person reading the page should feel like you are talking to them at that very moment. It may not seem like a big deal now, but writing something personal like this will be very important to your loved ones reading your letter in years to come.

To add an element of creativity to your layout, fold the letter in threes and adhere only the back of the middle third to the scrapbook page. This will give you more room in your layout, and it adds extra interest to the page where the reader has to unfold the note. You can also put the letter into an envelope that you fasten onto the page, allowing the reader to take the letter out of the envelope to read it.

CHAPTER 10
Lettering

As with any visual element, your scrapbook page needs something that will catch the reader's eye. Creative lettering will do just that. There are a lot of elements to lettering, ranging from computer fonts to developing your own unique artistic style. This chapter will explore the range of creative lettering possibilities.

What Is Creative Lettering?

Creative lettering is the incorporation of artistic elements to the alphabet. It's a technique that adds color and dimension to a scrapbook layout. Whether you simply add color to letters, embellish them with chalk, or add images to the traditional alphabet, creative lettering will unquestionably brighten your page.

The tools needed for creative lettering do not differ from the basic tools needed for scrapbooking. Rulers, pencils, and pens can be found in any scrapbook store. Remember to be sure that all of your materials are archival quality and permanent.

Pens will be the most expensive tools for lettering, and the large array of colors and tips will probably keep you coming back for more! Make sure you are comfortable using the different styles of pen tips. It's a good idea to practice using an assortment of pen thicknesses and strokes.

When doing any lettering, the general rule is to use twelve basic symbols to make all of your letters. These shapes, put together, create the alphabet. They are taken from the same elements that kindergarten teachers use to teach their children how to write. In fact, they are a standard element taught to potential teachers at the college level. As any schoolteacher will tell you, when learning for the first time, it is important to practice these shapes as you perfect your lettering techniques.

Lettering Symbols

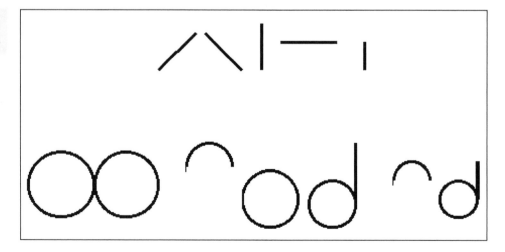

Practice makes perfect. Use the time when you are sitting in front of the television (or bored in an office meeting) to practice your lettering techniques. Use scrap paper and keep one or two journaling pens with you to get just the right touch.

Spacing

Lettering also means using a little engineering sense. Correctly spacing the title into your layout can make all of the difference to the overall look of the page. To be sure you get it down right, follow these simple steps to letter spacing.

1. Count the number of letters and spaces in the lettering title.
2. Divide that number by two.
3. Use that number to count to the middle of the space where you want your title to appear.
4. Mark on the layout with a light pencil where you want the center of the title.
5. Using a ruler and pencil, lightly mark the top and bottom (height) of the title.
6. Using a light pencil, draft the title starting with the middle of the text.
7. Backtrack to finish the beginning of the title.
8. Make sure all of the letters are evenly spaced.
9. Produce the final title using your selected pens and techniques.
10. Erase any remaining pencil marks.

Standard Lettering Styles

The basic lettering styles have the most common look and are also easy to produce. For every page that you embellish with a fancy lettering technique, you will most likely create four or five pages using standard letters. They are fast and almost effortless to make, and they look very nice.

Blocks and Bubbles

Block and bubble letters are very common and easy, but they do not provide as much definition or creativity as some of the other basic styles. For both block and bubble styles, you simply make the letter in a thick outline. However, the styles do differ in how they are created. For block letters, it is best to pick up your pen after each lettering symbol is stroked, while bubble letters should be completed using the same stroke for the whole letter. These styles can be embellished with chalk or other colors to jazz them up a bit.

QUESTIONS?

How do you create little holes in bubble letters?
Use a standard office hole-punch to create the effect of small holes in bubble titles for letters such as A, B, D, O, P, Q, and R.

Outlining Letters

Outlining letters is a quick lettering technique that provides definition and contrast to the scrapbook page. Draw the letter with a thick, even stroke throughout. Using a contrasting color, outline the letter evenly, making sure the outline is thinner than the stroke you used to draw the letter. Be aware of your spacing before you outline so you can decide whether you want the letters to touch each other.

Letter Filling

Filling letters is a basic style, but it takes a little more practice to perfect. It entails creating a block within the letter for another color. Only the straight part of the letter, however, should be filled to create this technique. For example, the straight part of an R, B, or J would be filled with a contrasting color, leaving the curved parts of these letters in the solid original color.

Fancy Frills

Crafting letters does not mean that you have to have any artistic abilities! Some easy letter embellishment techniques will make even the least artistic person look like a natural. Different tools can be used to adorn basic letters, including chalk, stickers, and markers, but overall it does not take many more instruments to create something that looks professional.

Only the Shadow Knows

Shadowing letters takes a little practice. Imagine that the sun is shining on the letter from the left and casting a shadow to the far, or right, side of the letter. Whatever direction your shadows go, the shadow on the letter should look like it is being cast from a light source shining from the opposite direction. If the light is coming from the left, then both curved and straight sections of your letter would be shadowed on the right. Simple forms of text are the easier to shadow. Using shadows on outlined or filled letters might create a look that's too busy for the page.

SSENTIALS

Clear rulers are most often used for creative lettering. They allow you to see where each letter is marked to begin and end. These are made of thick plastic and can be found in the scrapbooking section of your craft store.

The End Result

Adding an element to the end of letters is a common form of embellishment. From basic dots to more extravagant details that complement the theme of the page, letter endings are fairly quick and easy.

Text looks best with letter ends when it's written in all capital or all lowercase letters—instead of a mix of the two. It gives the embellishment consistency in the title. The process begins with using a basic letter that has no frills. Draw the letter onto your layout and space it accordingly. Make sure you give yourself enough room to effectively put an embellishment onto the end. Once all of the letters are done, go back and add the endings. As with most lettering, it is always best to draw your letters in pencil first to avoid any mistakes.

Divide or Unite

The same embellishments that were used for endings can also be used for separating the letters. This involves placing a small decoration or image in between your letters and still making them read as one word. Usually used with capital letters, the embellishment is generally not large and should be a complement to the theme of the page. For example, you might use hearts to separate the letters of a romantic page or daisies to separate letters in a spring layout.

Basic lettering styles

◆ • ◆ • ◆ • ◆

Using end, separation, and embellishments in lettering

The opposite of separating letters with images is to overlap letters within the title. This is a common practice and can be done for a fun effect or out of necessity to save room in a cramped layout spread. Most lettering styles can be used for overlapping or uniting letters, but be sure to make these decisions well in advance to account for any changes in an outline or filler. The one case when you should avoid using overlapping is on text that is shadowed. When these techniques are used together, the look they produce is awkward and busy.

Stuck on You

If you do not want to draw your own creative letters, try using letter stickers for scrapbook titles. They come in a variety of shapes, sizes, and colors, and they are easy to place onto the layout page. For a little embellishment, cut complementary patterned paper into a square with decorative scissors and then place the letter sticker in the middle of the cutout. Use the lettered squares to create the title, allowing it to be more creative and recognizable.

FACTS

Titles on magazine covers are lettered in color combinations that have been researched to stand out and be noticed. Stop by a newsstand the next time you are in a creative lettering slump to get some ideas!

While letter stickers are one way to avoid creative lettering on your own, stickers with images can play a completely different role in adorning the alphabet. Embellishing your own letters with stickers sometimes adds just the simple touch you were looking for, with the added benefit of making things very easy for you.

Using stickers on the entire title is often not necessary. One or two strategically placed stickers will usually be enough to get the style you are looking to achieve. Once the title is complete, deliberately place your stickers to allow them to hang on a letter or actually become the letter. It can be as much as a full daisy sticker (stem, leaves, and flower) to replace an "i", or as little as using a daisy as the dot for an "i". A star can replace an "O," and a crescent moon can complement a "C." Being inventive with your stickers in lettering can make them much more useful than just randomly scattering stickers throughout the page.

Color Me

Tools like colored pencils, chalk, and fancy markers will add a dimension of color and design to your lettering. Patterns and shading can be created with any of these materials. Find colors that complement the layout and use them within the letters.

When shading letters, instead of using black, try using a darker shade than that of the letter to complement it. For example, shade a pastel blue with a navy blue, or shade a red with a burgundy. Use chalk and blend together for a smooth finish, or for an even more creative look, use two colors and blend them towards the middle of the letter. Add patterns by randomly filling in dots, lines, or small images, or use colorful icons on the outside of letters to brighten up a page.

If you use color tools to embellish letters, you would be wise to mark the letters off of the layout page and add them when they are complete. This is to counter any mistakes since you generally cannot erase these embellishments. Consider making the creative lettering title on a piece of card stock that can be added later.

Alphabet Templates

Alphabet templates are popular among first-time scrappers. They seem to be easier than drawing freehand, and as an added bonus they guarantee a perfect lettered title. This may be true, but many find that freehand lettering eventually becomes more natural and less bothersome than using a template.

SSENTIALS

Practice using your Exacto knife with scrap before you use it on traced letters. Always use a mat to prevent any damage to your tabletop. As a general rule, it helps to maintain a steady hand if you carefully cut toward you, and for a cleaner incision, turn the paper instead of the blade when cutting curves.

When tracing titles, be sure to use a pencil to first get down the letters onto your page. Stenciling though the template with a pen or marker will blot the template itself by bleeding onto the bottom. It will also smear onto your page if you lift it before the ink has dried. This can slow you down because after you outline each letter you have to wait to lift the template.

Plastic templates are not as easy to use if you plan on cutting out the letters after they are traced. Stencils often have intricate angles and tiny details that make them difficult and frustrating to cut out. If you absolutely must cut out the letters, use a micro-scissors to get deep into the angles or try an Exacto knife with a sharp blade.

Festive Fonts

Fonts in layouts are becoming more and more popular in scrapbooking. Your own writing is already being manipulated in creative lettering, so the theory that you must use your own handwriting for memory's sake does not apply. The authenticity or personal nature of the text is already diminished for the sake of creative expression, so computer fonts are an excellent alternative.

Lettering fonts

◆ ◆ ◆ ◆ ◆ ◆

Using fonts to add creative lettering

Kringle
LD Billboard
Girls Are Weird
Hippo Critic
KA MONSTER
PAINT BOY
Smiley
TENDER
TOOL SHOP CAPS

There are thousands of fonts that will provide beautiful titles and lettering for your layouts. If you have a color printer, the choices then become even better. Downloading fonts from the Internet is easy, and most sites that offer free fonts also post a step-by-step guide.

Computer software is now available that allows a high level of inventiveness in set fonts. Some programs come with dozens of fonts and over 600 lettering graphics. This variety will allow you to manipulate words and letters to fit your specific needs. Techniques such as the ability to change the fill-color in each letter or to flip letters into reverse are all advantages to purchasing a specialty program.

Standard word processing programs are most popular in lettering. The "Word Art" program allows you a great deal of creativity with little effort. The Word Art gallery allows you to select from thirty styles of word images to display your text. Once this is selected, you can then choose from forty styles of text shape as well as features for color, shade, grade, texture, pattern, transparency, or rotation.

Creating Your Own Letters

The task of creating your own form of letters is intimidating. Many scrappers do not even give this a try. However, inventing your own letters can also be fun and rewarding. Scrapbook pages that contain these personal creations will become some of your more cherished layouts.

Check your spelling of the title before using your creative lettering techniques! If you do make a mistake, leave it in and add a small "oops" near the word. You might think it embarrassing now, but your great-grandchildren will probably get a kick out of it!

If you break down each letter into the symbols that make them up, the process becomes much easier. For example, a J is broken down into three parts: a bottom curve, a vertical straight line, and a horizontal straight line. After the letter is broken down, make a list of possible theme-related items. Once your list is complete, compare the items to see how you might possibly combine them in the lettering. If the subject was baseball, your list might include a baseball hat, baseball bat, and baseball. Visualizing these items into the letter then becomes much easier.

Personalized lettering using the letter J

The Title Page

Creative lettering means producing page titles. Many of us labor over titles because we think the final decision will make or break a page. Ultimately, the title is the first thing that readers see when they look through your album. Creating titles should not be as difficult as it looks. Instead of thinking that your title will define the page, think about how it could complement the page and use it accordingly.

Catchy and rhyming phrases are the best source of titles, as are common sayings or clichés. The title "Dalton Turns One" is effective for a birthday page, but using the title "Cute as a Bun at One!" instead adds some enthusiasm to the layout. Nursery rhymes and famous movie names are also practical and amusing page titles.

As you hear interesting phrases that you think might be good to use in a future page, jot them down in your journal or notepad. These are great resources when you are having trouble thinking of a title. It is also good to have these with you as you visit a scrapbooking store. The title you intend to use will have influence on the materials you purchase to create your layout, including colors and decorative papers.

ESSENTIALS

Old postcards and greeting cards are good resources for ideas on both creative lettering and titles. These are also good resources for ideas about color and design for your layout! Stash them away in an old gift bag or a bottom drawer, but keep a reminder near your scrapbooking workstation to turn to them for inspiration.

Thinking of titles might drive you crazy, especially if you cannot seem to find the one that is right for your page. Consider posting a question on an Internet scrapbooking board asking for suggestions. Chances are you will get a lot of responses.

Local crops are a perfect resource for finding suggestions for titles. Pass around a paper with your theme and ask for everyone's ideas. For incentive, turn it into a contest awarding something small to the person whose title you choose. The prize should not be expensive and could be as simple as some punch-outs from one of your most treasured punches.

CHAPTER 11

Border Patrol

As with any artistic creation or picture, a surrounding frame will complement both the colors and style of the element involved. Scrapbook pages are no exception. Borders also allow the scrapbook page to look final and complete. This chapter will discuss the styles of scrapbook page borders and how to be unique in your page border selection.

Basic Borders

Framing a page is a basic way to use a border in scrapbooking. Created from elements of roughly the same sizes, these frames are most common and can be fairly uncomplicated if you want to produce some quick results. A border that runs the entire edge of your page should be small or thin, leaving you enough room to produce your layout. Thicker borders often take into account elements of the layout overlapping the frame.

Choosing Sides

Borders do not have to be equally represented on all four sides of your scrapbook page. Use a vertical border to allow a design to run up and down one side of the page. It changes the composition of the page, making it appear thinner, and it automatically creates a vertical movement in the layout. Images are often used in borders to portray a repetitive element. It is fun to use one large image that runs up and down a vertical borders, such as a balloon, airplane, or lollipop.

Action images in a border consist of one object moving along the paper edge. Examples include a stroller on a sidewalk, a car driving on the road, a rocket ship blasting off, or a bird soaring to a birdhouse.

Horizontal borders on a scrapbook page run on the top or bottom of the page, or both. Framing the layout in this fashion allows you to continue a left-to-right movement if you desire. Borders that run in the same direction as we read are best to use if you want to produce a title border or a border that includes some journaling elements. Action images in these borders should flow horizontally, creating movement on the page.

Creative Options

The four corners are popular place to embellish in order to maintain a border look for your page. They often do not connect to one another, but the presence of designs in these four equal areas visually allows for a simulated border effect. You can decorate your corners using simple corner punches, but designs created from attractive papers and decorative scissors will add a unique touch to the page. Images copied to each corner are common, as are small elements hugging the corners to form a repetitive bond.

Borders running both pages will complement a two-page design. It allows for a flow across the spread that combines the two pages into one element. These styles of borders will additionally act as a catalyst for movement across the two pages. A frame border joins all of the outside edges of a page to define it as one large layout. Vertical borders on the outside edge of each page bring the elements of the layout towards the middle.

Border Tips

You might read scrapbooking tips on the Internet or other resources that suggest creating your borders after the layout is in place. If this instruction is not explained well, you might interpret it meaning you should adhere all materials to the page and then add the border as a finishing touch. Borders do give the page a finished look, but you should decide on your border during the process of creating the layout. Borders make a bold statement and change the dynamics of a page, and therefore you should determine your border style while you are creating the page composition.

SSENTIALS

Drawing a straight line with a light pencil will help to keep your depth and angles in line. Whether it is as simple as a straight paper border, or as detailed as a wavy design created from decorative materials, this preliminary pencil line will be your guide to ensuring equal depth throughout the length of the border.

When creating a border, lay out the page design to decide what kind of border will complement the page composition. This way you can tell what size and style of page frame you need. It will also help if you determine at this stage whether you are going to use a horizontal angle, vertical angle, or frame the entire page. A light pencil marking where the elements of the page are arranged will also help once the style of border is determined.

Page Dividers

On the interior of pages, borders make a good way of showing two different elements on one page or of designing a before-and-after effect. These page separators cannot officially be called borders, since a border is defined as an edge, but they do work in the same way as actual borders in that they run the length of a page.

Using a page divider

Dividing a page in half vertically does not allow for much room on an 8.5" × 11" scrapbook page. Halving the page horizontally is easier and produces a nice effect. If you do want to divide a page in half, try using a 12" × 12" scrapbook page to allow for adequate room on each side. For best results, consider separating the page diagonally. It creates an artistic feel, and the length and variety of the page break or border increases.

Scrapbook pages devoted to a "That was then, this is now" theme are fun to divide, especially for pages depicting two stages in a person's life. Scrapbooking a picture on the first day of school of kindergarten and then on graduation day is a perfect reason to divide the page.

Other uses for page division include comparing photos of ancestors with today's generation, particularly if you can find a picture of the two generations doing the same thing. For example, the two halves of the scrapbook page might show a great-grandfather and a great-grandson each playing baseball, with a sports border complementing and drawing the elements together.

Shapes Up!

You can use common shapes as a basic tool for creating border designs. Shapes offer a complement to the layout, a contrast with each other, and can give a nice look to your pattern. A basic border might repeat one shape for the length of the page or use a variety of shapes in a particular configuration.

Standard 12" × 12" album pages are often not a true twelve inches vertically or horizontally. Measure your album page before cutting materials to create a page border or divider.

Create designs using the shapes in order (triangle, circle, square, triangle, circle, square, and so forth), overlapping one another on the ends, or on top of each other. For example, cut out a square, place a slightly smaller circle on top of it in a contrasting color, and then place a smaller triangle in the same color as the original square. Continue to create these patterns and place them one after another onto your scrapbook page for a border.

Borders using
basic shapes

Squares cut with decorative scissors are a common shape for creating borders. Use a color that complements the layout, particularly one that might be used for a picture mat. As you place the squares onto the border, slightly overlap them, turning each one so that they do not make a straight line. It might look as if the squares are dancing on the page.

Paper Décor

Decorative paper is frequently used for creating borders. Sometimes the paper is already equipped with a border that you can use as a full page or cut to complement other parts of the layout. Decorative papers are popular to use as photo mats, and many brands make flattering paper styles that would complement a border. These often contain the same base color but offer a different looking texture on the page itself.

Patterned papers are also great to cut into shapes and can make a nice contrast to an otherwise mundane page. Cut them in slivers and overlap them to create a woven border, or use a scrapbooking tool like a punch to jazz up otherwise common objects that create your border.

SSENTIALS If possible, try to purchase two sheets of each style of decorative paper in case you use it for a two-page spread or border. Patterns are constantly being replaced in stores with more current, trendier items. It can be hard to match a pattern that you purchased months earlier.

Framing a page with patterned pages can be difficult in two-page spreads. Consider using half of the page on one side and the other half on the opposite, partially framing the layout. You might use the pattern in a border on the top right hand corner and run it three-quarters down the side, and then continue the same idea on the bottom left hand corner, only this time running the border three-quarters up the side. This will create a diagonal frame effect and capture the paper on each page for consistency.

The Border Line

Simple lines are frequently used as scrapbooking borders, often created by easy-to-use template systems. As with most scrapbook techniques, always begin your project in pencil so you can fix any mistakes that might occur.

Products on the market that assist in creating line borders come in all shapes and sizes and are easy to use. Sometimes in the form of a ruler, the template will have measurement markings on one side and a trace-able design outlined on the other.

FACTS

A Border Buddy is a template especially made to assist in the creation of scrapbook page borders. They come in a variety of styles, including seasonal, romantic, geometric, and beach. These are popular items can be found at local scrapbooking stores and, for a few pennies less, on Internet retail sites.

The best templates to use for line borders are square, with different outline designs cut into each side. Additionally, you can stencil from cutouts on the inside of the template with shapes that often complement the border designs. For example, a wavy romantic border template might have a heart stencil inside that you can use along with the frame.

When creating lines, consider the various looks that different tips of acid-free pens will make on the page. The width of the pen or marker thoroughly changes the look of the design. A thicker marker might not be appropriate for more intricate outlines, as the details could easily get lost. On the contrary, borders drawn with thin lines could be too dainty for a hearty-looking page.

Craft punches and rubber-stamping are two scrapbooking techniques that can be a tremendous asset to border art. Learn about these methods for many options in creating unique page frames.

Creativity in line borders lies in the products you intend to use. A template is a perfect tool for creating more than one border line on the same side of the page. Simply move the border stencil off center from the original line. Do this a few times, and allow the lines to create a pattern. Most of these border templates will also have a corner stencil to make creative angles. Permit the lines to flow into these corners for a slick-looking frame.

Using templates also can spark some creativity in the concept of some border designs. You might have a wavy-edged template that would easily lend itself to creating basic curvy lines or drawing an ocean border. If you use some more imaginative methods, you can then create something completely different. Instead of an ocean, you might use the "wave" feature to create dinosaur scales or a cactus plant. Use only portions of the border and flip it to generate an opposite effect.

Border Materials

The use of stickers in borders is common and will give you a great deal of flexibility in creating your layout pages. Stickers add color and variety, and they will save you time if you do not want to put the work into designing an elaborate page frame.

Border stickers are made in standard page-length sheets, enabling you to simply stick a ready-made border onto the page. Brands such as Provo Craft offer a large variety of styles. They often produce border strips with clear backing, allowing you to effectively mount the stickers on a complementary color card stock.

Often used to form a repetitive border, stickers might be placed one after another on a complementary background for the length of the paper edge. Stickers can also be used to tell a story in the border, placing different designs next to each other. For example, instead of placing a strip of teddy bears to border a baby page, you might use all different kinds of baby stickers including a pacifier, bottle, diaper, blanket, etc.

Border stickers can really pop out when they are mounted on the same materials as your pictures. As long as the stickers do not get lost in the style of patterned paper or a on a backing that is too dark to accommodate them, the stickers extract an element of continuity from using the same mat materials.

Fun Border Art

The standard repetitive border, shapes repeated along a page edge, can be broken up every few pages by using a fun and easy technique to emphasize originality. These may take a little more time to complete, but the end result is worth the effort.

Stretched Text

Using words in your borders is common, where they can act as a page title as well. A frequently used bit of border art stems from using one word that relates to the theme and stretching it across the page. Once that is complete, a phrase relevant to the page focus is stretched across the middle of the larger word. This usually is done in cursive writing if both elements are drawn by hand directly onto the page, but can also be done using a WordArt program on your computer.

Using
WordArt
for borders

Use Your Creativity

Emphasizing
one element
of an image
to produce a
page border

Border ends are another way you can use your creative skills to design something little more artistic than a standard line border. Border ends are created in much the same way as lettering ends, including placing a design on the edge of each border. Flowers, stars, hearts, and other basic images are all common in border ends, but a little creativity can really make your page stand out. For example, instead of a basic Easter egg repetitive border, you might have a slightly wavy line of grass topped with a bunny, with border ends as colored Easter eggs.

Another way to be creative in your border is to caricature one portion of your image to exaggerate it. Cartoon the image by drawing it out of proportion. These are often used in vertical borders, allowing components of an image to be stretched. For example, using the same Easter theme, you might have a border with a bunny rabbit whose ears stretch all of the way to the top of the page.

Unique Borders

There is a small difference between making an artistic border and creating a unique border. Both look for the development of a design or image that will stand out or complement the layout. Unique borders, however, might use elements that are uncommon for the daily scrapper, or materials so exclusive that they are used only one time in your album.

Mulberry Paper Borders

Mulberry and other handmade papers are popular ways of creating rough edge border. Borders that play into the effect of an entire page scene, such as snow drifts or beach sand, look more realistic with a rugged edge. Mulberry paper can be torn to create these wispy and uneven effects.

Be careful with colorfast or dye fabrics! If used in the scrapbook page, they might bleed onto other areas of the layout. Consider washing fabrics before using them as a border in your layout.

In very light pencil, design your border onto the paper. With a small wet cotton swab, trace over these thin lines. Before the wet line dries, apply pressure to hold down one side of the page while gently tugging on the other. This will break the page at the uneven wet mark and create the rough-edged border you are seeking.

Quilt Borders

Quilting borders in your layout will have many of the same qualities as the quilt scrapbook page discussed in Chapter 13. The rules to border quilting, however, are more relaxed and allow for freedom in the design. It is a great style to use when you need to clean out your scrap drawer!

Quilt borders can incorporate a sense of organization, such as maintaining a pattern of angled decorative papers or stabilizing the frame with the same colored corners. For the most part, however, creating a quilt border simply means forming angled papers around the edge of the scrapbook page to create a frame for the layout. To jazz up the look even more, use a black acid-free fine-tip pen to mark each paper with "stitching" around the edge.

Uncommon Border Materials

The materials used in a border can also allow for quite a unique creation. Fabric is thought to be acid free, and used in the layout it will add a special look to the page. Scraps of fabric can be put together for a quilted look, or a strip might be used on just one side.

String can also be used if you are creating a hidden journaling layout in the border. Punch a hole into the journaling page and thread thin string through each paper and loosely tie at the end. Once this is complete, adhere the backing of the journaling paper to the scrapbook page.

This style is particularly nice when you might have extra materials from an outfit made for a son or daughter. If the pictures in the layout include the child wearing these clothes, the exact match in corresponding fabric will be a perfect addition to the scrapbook page.

Another material that is often used to create unique borders is string. Popular images such as kites, balloons, or lollipops will stand out a great deal more if you use a real string instead of drawing a two-dimensional image.

Border Stories

Many scrappers rely on the area in the picture frame to tell the story and save the middle of the page for groupings of pictures. Some of the more unique pages are expressive enough that they do not need a title or words, simply allow the images on the picture frame do the talking. Whether this style is effective or not, it is unique and worth a try. For example, in a page depicting pictures from a child's first steps, you might begin the border with stickers of a baby sitting, move next to stickers of a baby crawling, and finish with stickers of a baby standing or walking. The images on the border clearly depict the sentiments of the layout itself.

FACTS

Artists use matting to border their work and enable them to pull certain colors out as a visual effect. They often rely on this element of framing to take one color that might not have been as prominent and extract it by choosing a similar color to border the work.

Actually telling the story through words in a border is also an option for some very unique pages. Draw a large enough square border around the page to write your thoughts, or take a more creative step and design a border book. To do this, create room for a two-inch border on one side of your layout. Cut two pieces of card two and a half inches wide, with the length depending on the size of the album and whether you're using a vertical or horizontal border. One piece of card stock should be white and the other, which will be the top page, a color or decorative paper that will complement the layout. Fold the top paper back one-quarter inch, and adhere this small edge to the white card stock. This will create a book effect in your border and allow you room to journal on the white paper. Once it is complete, adhere the entire border book to the layout.

CHAPTER 12

Scrapbooking Techniques

As you continue your journey through the craft of scrapbooking, you might find yourself getting bored with the basic tools and techniques frequently used by beginners. While beginner steps are at the heart of scrapbooking, creative techniques will stimulate you into producing fun and lively layouts.

The Color Wheel

The color wheel is a way of looking at color that allows you to creatively use colors to enhance and complement one another. It is made up of the three primary colors (red, blue, and yellow) and the three secondary colors (green, orange, and violet). In the color wheel, each secondary color is placed in between two primary colors.

Six tertiary colors are then created by combining a primary color with one of the secondary colors bordering it. This arrangement is not particular to scrapbooking: it's an ancient way of looking at color that is used by artists in every genre. Chances are you learned about this in an art class growing up.

The Color
Wheel

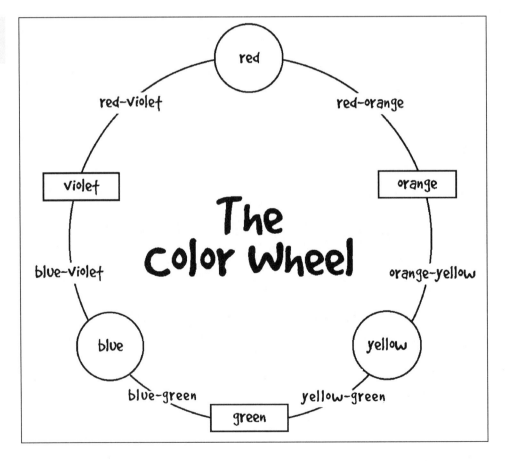

Using a basic artistic tool like the color wheel in scrapbooking is a way to ensure that colors will complement each other. The colors that are directly opposite from one another are very flattering when used in the same layout, making each look intensified.

FACTS

Color blocking is a technique that applies a section of contrasting color to your scrapbook layout. Usually divided into two or four sections, a different base color would be used for backing in the top and bottom of a page, on either side, or to divide it into quadrants.

The color wheel is most useful in the way its arrangement separates colors. Analogous colors, for example, are separated by just one color on the color wheel. They cooperate with each other by using one of the same colors and therefore will complement each other in a layout. For example, if you use the primary color blue for your ocean, analogous (and tertiary) colors blue-green and blue-violet would be excellent choices to complement the layout in photo mats or borders. Terms that describe spacing and combinations of color in the color wheel include:

Adjacent Colors—Colors that fall next to each other on the color wheel.
Analogous Colors—Colors that are separated by one color on the color wheel.
Brown—The combination of all three primary colors.
Complementary Colors—Opposite each other on the color wheel.
Double Complement—A layout using two sets of complementary colors.
Harmony—Using any three colors that are side by side on a color wheel in a scrapbook page. Monochromatic Color Scheme—A variation of one color (for example, different shades of navy blue).
Split Complementary Color Scheme—Using three colors, one primary and two tertiary, that fall adjacent to the primary color's complement.
Triadic Color Scheme—Using three colors evenly spaced on the color wheel.
Tetrad Color Scheme—Using four colors that are evenly spaced on the color wheel.

Scrapbook Stamping

One of the most popular techniques to come out of scrapbooking is stamping. Started as a companion craft to the creation of homemade paper decorations and cards, stamping is fun to use on scrapbook layouts in designs and borders.

Tools of the Trade

Stamps come in all shapes, sizes, and designs. Most have a wooden base with a rubber stamp image adhered to it. For ease in finding the stamp you are looking for, or to help line it up on a page, many brands provide the picture of the stamp on the top of the wooden base.

Using a stamp to complement a scrapbook page

Rubber stamps are sold individually at craft supply stores or at local scrapbooking stores. Direct sales companies have begun to broaden the stamping market through home shows, which are similar to home scrapbooking shows. Depending on the size of the stamp, costs run from $2 per stamp to $30 for a stamping kit. Kits will include a series of stamps in the same theme, as well as one or two inkpads. These are useful if you want diversity in the images you are expressing through stamping while still keeping the same general theme.

Inkpads are the second tool necessary for scrapbook stamping. They come in a few different styles. Dye inkpads are made with a water base. Instead of inking the scrapbook paper, they will basically leave a dye-stain on the material in the form of the die shape.

This water-based ink is easy to clean from rubber stamps and dries very quickly on the layout design, allowing little room for human error with smudging. The water solution, however, does put the dye-ink designs at greater risk of running if they get wet after the project is complete.

QUESTIONS?

What is a die?
A die is the raised rubber part of a stamp that captures the image.

Pigment inkpads allow more flexibility in scrapbooking because the colors offered are more brilliant and lively. They have color particles included in the base ink, giving us a diverse selection of interesting shades. It also means the ink is less likely to be affected or damaged by water. Pigment ink is prone to smudging because it stays wet longer, but it is also ideal for the embossing technique, which relies on wet ink to be successful.

The final tool you need for stamping is a liquid that will clean a stamp surface of ink. These cleaning solutions are especially important if you intend to use pigment and permanent dyes. They are nontoxic and water based and can be purchased for a few dollars from a craft store. Household items that also work well include baby-wipes and premoistened cleaning wipes.

Stamping Application

Applying rubber stamps to a scrapbook page does not take a lot of explanation, but it does take some practice. To begin, ink the rubber die with the inkpad of your choice. Pads are usually raised above their plastic holder, allowing you to ink the entire die evenly. Once each protruding portion is well inked, carefully press it onto the selected paper.

A "stamping positioner" is a tool that helps you to evenly position your stamp onto the page. Positioners are helpful, but more often than not scrapbookers find it easier to simply attempt correct spacing with a careful look and a little intuition. Use light pencil lines to help create even borders, and mark the page to show where other items will be laid out.

FACTS

Permanent inks are water resistant. They are used on atypical surfaces in scrapbooks, such as thin sheets of plastic, glass, or wood, which are sometimes used in a special page or technique.

It is very important that you maintain even pressure on the stamp, using your palm to keep it level. A common mistake in stamping applications is to rock the stamp back and forth. This creates an uneven look, and it will sometimes create a double image if the stamp is moved slightly as it rocks. Practice a few times before you stamp your final product.

Once you have applied even pressure, lift the stamp straight up from the page. Lifting it on an angle toward you might produce a smudge, or you might catch another section of the page and produce an unwanted mark. If you do make a mistake, use materials such as stickers, die-cuts, other stamping, or journaling to cover the error instead of scrapping the page all together.

Coloring Stamps

The most obvious way to color your images is to use a colored stamp pad. These often come in a rainbow of different hues that includes metallic colors, autumn colors, or pastels. Stamp pads can also be found in individual colors and sizes.

You can color your images with any of the basic acid-free materials found at the scrapbook store. One of the more popular items is a brush-tip marker. These fancy pens are usually noted with a "BR" on the cap of the pen where the tip grade is normally marked. These pens allow for flexibility in how you accent the image. They can often save you money by eliminating the need to purchase several different tips in the same color.

Fine-tip pens are good resources for filling in small areas like flower petals. Medium-tipped pens are of a helpful size for accenting stamp edges. On the other hand, gel-rollers might seem like a fun alternative, but the pen flow is sometimes difficult to control and the ink might seep onto the stamp edges, covering the lines.

As with all scrapbooking materials, the colors that you use to surround an image will also have a bearing on the way the figure is perceived. Cool colors will give it a calming look, while bold colors makes the image more active. To enhance this, consider using chalk or colored pencils inside the stamped image to complement the surrounding colors.

ESSENTIALS

Store all ink pads in an sealed freezer bag. Before closing the bag, be sure that all of the air has been removed and the items are airtight. Even though most ink pads do come with a lid, this is not enough to keep them from drying out.

One of the more creative ways to add color to your stamping is by using watercolor techniques. This hand-painted look can be accomplished by either using watercolor paints or watercolor pencils.

Paints are no different than the basic watercolors you used in school. They are inexpensive and easy to use. Practice on some scrap paper so you can see how to make the watercolors darker and also to get a sense of how to control the flow of water and paint from the brush.

A watercolor pencil, on the other hand, is likely to be a material that you have never used. They basically give the same look of watercolors, but the process starts by using specialty colored pencils. To use, fill in the stamped image with your choice of colored pencil. Use a fine wet paintbrush to then go over the colored areas to create the watercolor look. Be careful with both of these styles of watercolor—pigment-based inks should be used in stamping to prevent any running.

Embossing

Embossing is a stamping technique, but its unique qualities put it in a category of its own category. The term *emboss* means to decorate with raised designs and patterns. You have probably noticed embossed items ranging from cards to heritage frames. If you run your finger over an embossed item, you will feel the pattern raised from the surface in lines and bumps.

Heat Embossing

Embossing is based on the technique of rubber stamping. To emboss in your scrapbook, you will first need to understand the method of rubber stamping. Pigment stamping ink is necessary to emboss, and in sufficient quantity so that the ink will stay wet on the page for a few seconds. After stamping, drizzle a material called embossing powder onto the wet image. This is similar to how you might sprinkle glitter onto white glue.

Embossing powder will be on the paper in more of a quantity than you need, and it is important to remove the excess before you take the next step. Carefully knock the edge of the paper on its side to allow some of the powder to fall off the surface. If this is not safe for your page, use a small dry paintbrush to brush excess away.

Heat-emboss on card stock separate from photographs. The intense heat may damage pictures beyond repair. Add the stamped figure after embossing to ensure saving all of your memories on the page.

When the surface is free from excess powder, the only embossing powder remaining will be sticking to the ink of your stamped image. Use an embossing heat gun to heat the image. Found at any scrapbooking or stamping store, this tool acts on the embossing powder to cause the image to become glossy and rise in about 30 seconds. Be sure not to use the heat gun for any longer than 30 seconds or until the image becomes glossy. Too much heat can be detrimental to a stamped figure and cause dullness or even ruin the base paper.

Also be aware of where your fingers are during the heating process. Embossing images on small scraps could put your fingers too close to the heat gun and cause a burn. If this is a possibility, use a pair of kitchen tongs to hold the paper while it is being heated.

Embossing Options

Blind embossing, the easiest of the embossing techniques, uses prefabricated materials with raised designs already intact. You might also blind emboss by using a prefabricated press to make the impression. These are specialized items and can be found at franchise craft superstores and local scrapbooking stores. They may be harder to locate in a small general craft store. They are fun to use for picture frames or photo mounts, especially with heritage or other black and white photos.

Embossing pens are yet another option. These come in clear or an entire collection of colors. You might use them to draw on clip art, outline die-cuts, highlight creative lettering, or embellish photo mounting. Embossing pens work on the same principle as embossed stamped images. The pen leaves wet ink on the page in whatever line or design you draw with it. You then sprinkle embossing powder on the area that you want embossed, brush off the excess powder, and finish with the embossing heat gun.

Punch Art

Paper punching is an almost addictive technique that eventually attracts most scrapbookers. It used to be a very simple craft that created embellishments for small areas of a page or for border art. But within the last several years, craft companies have begun manufacturing punches with more intricate and interesting images than basic swirls, hearts, stars, and circles.

Along with new shapes such as lightning bolts, teddy bears, and snowflakes, you can now find very specific images such as oak leaves, acorns, paw prints, mailboxes, cars, and baby bottles. And that's just to name a few. Crafters who found these unique punches also realized that images could easily be cut or modified to create something completely new. With this the art form of paper punching began.

Example of punch art

Punch art can get very intricate and detailed, and there are several books on the market hundreds of pages long that describe individual punch artistic techniques. For a beginner, however, this example will serve to show how you can use basic and common punch shapes to create a design.

This depiction of punch art forms an arrow shot into a tree. It uses the basic punch images of a star, heart, swirl, and snowflake. Both a large star and small star have been cut to form an arrow head, and snowflakes have been cut to allow portions of the snowflake to be used as arrow parts. To allow for the simulation tree leaves, large swirl punch-outs have been scattered randomly.

Paper Piecing

Paper piecing is the art of making figures and designs through patching different shapes together. They will add depth to a scrapbook page because of the layering style within the image. Pieced-paper figures look more mobile and three-dimensional.

The Art of Piecing

The art of piecing images together has a lot of help from scrapbook companies and Web sites who provide templates for this technique. A piecing template might have images of a coat, hat, boots, umbrella, face, eyes, and hands on one page. To begin the piecing process, a lightbox tool will allow you to trace these figures onto the paper or card stock of your choice. Trace them with a light pencil onto the backside of the paper, enabling you to cut the pieces without needing to erase any pencil marks.

Once you cut all of the pieces, place the fragments of the figure together to form the image. These templates are fun to use and can help with ideas. You will quickly find that piecing is not difficult, and you might find that creating your own piecing ideas can be a fun craft.

Use a photocopier to enlarge a piecing pattern. This will allow you to make an image larger to furnish a different layout or a two-page spread. For even larger images, use the legal paper section of the photocopier to fit all of your pieces.

Some kits found in scrapbooking stores provide all of the pieces and suggestions for the formation of an image. They are fun tools to use on your scrapbook page, and they do not take a lot of time to put together.

Making Your Own Pattern

Patterns for paper piecing do not have to come from ready-made templates. Any image can be formatted to a paper piecing artwork. Some popular places to find images to piece are coloring books, clip art, children's story books, magazines, animated video cassette cases, and Web sites.

If you decide to make your own paper-piecing pattern, take a few steps to perfect your technique. First, make sure that the pattern is not too detailed and that only a few pieces need to be created to put the image together. You can also cut out all of the parts in the template and use a pencil to outline them on the paper that you want to use for the image. Make sure that every piece is accounted for, and store the pattern in a marked envelope for future use.

Putting the Pieces Together

Once you have all the pieces cut out, adhering them together can be very laborious. There are sometimes so many little parts that you might need a keen eye to get it just right. An easy way to adhere these small pieces successfully is to glue the pieces first from the uppermost piece down to the lowest section. Follow these simple directions:

1. Decide where on the layout you would like to place the pattern.
2. Put all of the pieces in place without any glue.
3. Starting with the top piece, glue each piece to the one just beneath it.
4. Allow the entire piece to dry.
5. Embellish with chalk, colored pencil, or pen lines hugging the edge.
6. Affix to the layout page.

Piecing is not limited to basic paper shapes. A variety of materials will add depth to your page. Use fabric to depict dress materials or yarn as a dog leash. Specialty papers, such as mulberry or vellum, also make a nice change for your piecing art.

Paper piecing created from a stamping design

To add an even more artistic element to your piecing, use different patterned papers and colors for each different piecing shape. Make the legs different patterns or use a deep color umbrella with a pastel raincoat. Additionally, use brush pens, chalk, or colored pencils to add some flash to the art.

FACTS

The Internet is paper-piecing heaven for scrapbookers addicted to the art. There are hundreds of Web sites that offer free patterns and encourage you to copy the ideas. Be sure to check out the Web site appendix in this book to get started finding free samples.

Encapsulation

The term encapsulation seems daunting, mysterious, and even difficult. In reality, this is a technique that needs little explanation. Simply put, it is a process by which you can save heritage papers, clippings, or other types of souvenirs that you want in a completely archival environment. Encapsulation will prevent any harmful acidic materials from migrating to the important document.

To proceed with this technique, you will first need to use a deacidification spray on your paper materials paper (not on your photos) and wait for them to dry. Other material requirements include two sheets of Mylar or polypropylene plastic and double-sided tape.

ALERT

Laminating is a process of heating plastic onto an item and can easily ruin that item through heat and chemical aging. If you are interested in laminating an item to fulfill a certain look for your layout, consider making a color copy of the item before lamination and storing the original in a protective environment.

Place the document or picture in between these materials so that there is enough plastic material on each side for adhesive. On the edges, place double stick tape in between the plastic and seal. Be sure that the tape is far enough away from the encapsulated item, usually about ⅙ of an inch. This will protect your documents from handlers and moisture, but be aware that it will not shield against heat or fire.

The plastic used in encapsulation materials is called film. It generally comes in a few styles including gloss, matte, or satin finishes. The finish style usually depends on film thickness. There are up to five choices of film thickness, but this much variety can be hard to find. You might only find one or two choices of thickness at the local scrapbooking store. Thin grades of plastic are ideal for folding materials after they are encapsulated, but the more you intend the encapsulated item to be handled by others, the thicker the film should be.

Many encapsulating products come in prefabricated protective sleeves to hold items such as first teeth, locks of hair, or other awkwardly shaped memorabilia. For items such as a lock of hair, tie a ribbon around it and glue the ribbon to a paper backing before encapsulating it in the pouch.

Craft companies use the encapsulating process to enable you to use a material that might have otherwise been considered unsafe. For example, wood materials contain lignin, a highly acidic material. Deacidification sprays generally do not work on these materials and they are normally considered unfit for your scrapbook album. Some companies, such as Paper Adventures, have created wood products that are encapsulated and sealed without letting the look of the plastic film overpower the material. These materials are called WoodStock, and can be found in sheets as thin as card stock pages.

Chalk It Up!

The technique of chalking has gained popularity lately and has resulted in classes offered at local scrapbooking stores. This method became well liked for coloring instead of more expensive embellishments like specialty papers and markers. Chalk now comes in a variety of bold colors. It's come a long way from the standard pastels that we used in grade school. It is very important that your chalk is acid-free. Most standard artist's chalk is not archival quality. You should not purchase it unless it says "acid-free" on the box.

Chalk Application

You might remember using chalk sticks in grade school. The application process for the scrapbook, however, is a little different. There is no need for chalk getting all over your fingers by holding a chalk stick, in fact, using your hands is not recommended at all. Some people might try to encourage the use of your fingers for setting the chalk in place, or to blend two colors together. In truth, the oils on your hands can get onto the paper or chalk and change the look that you had intended.

Chalking Tools

There are tools on the market that are designed for the single purpose of applying chalk. Many look like a standard cotton swab with a small end and a flat end, and some look like cosmetic application sponges. This will allow variety in determining which applicator will be best for a particular image.

FACTS

A chalk eraser is a light colored eraser that will allow you to remove chalking errors without damaging your paper. They are soft and clearly marked especially for chalking, and can be found in the chalking section of any local scrapbooking or craft retail outlet.

While applicators are not too expensive, they will cost you more than using a standard cotton swab. Cotton swabs are ideal if you ensure that they will not result in too many cotton fragments on the page. To help avoid this, wet the cotton swab and allow it to dry overnight. By the next day you will have a chalk applicator that does not contain the fine particles that can sometimes cause chalking problems.

Another tool that might be helpful for chalking is a fixative spray. This mist will help adhere the chalk to the page, particularly if you do not use protective sleeves in your albums. To spray, hold the spout about eight inches above the page and lightly mist the material so the fixative drifts down onto the image. Some scrappers use hairspray as a fixative, but this is not recommended and can damage your layout materials.

Chalking Tips

- To shadow, use a darker shade of the colored item you want to shadow.
- Add a brush of water after chalking for a wispy look.
- Use a gel pen to write over chalk.
- Blend the edge where two colors meet to create a flow within the colors.
- Use matte paper for best results in chalking.
- Detail the edge of the chalked object with ink dashes for a "stitched" look.
- Scrape chalk dust onto a palette and combine with other colors to create your own shades.
- Use a dry artist paintbrush as an alternative to other application tools.
- Chalk the edge of die-cuts for embellishment.
- Use a dark background with light chalk for a bold layout.

CHAPTER 13

Artistic Creations

As you learn techniques for scrapbooking, it is easy to get an itch to create more artistic embellishments in your layouts. Learning popular techniques is only one option for scrapbooking enthusiasts—there are several types of artistic elements that go beyond the basics to beautify album pages.

Pop-Ups

If you remember the books you loved when you were younger, chances are a pop-up book is included in the list. They are fascinating for children and really stand out among the rest. Using the same technique in a scrapbook page can both add an element of surprise and cause whatever you are trying to express to dramatically stand out.

Pop-Up Instability

The most popular style of scrapbook pop-up extends over the top of a two-page layout. It is designed so that when you open the page, the pop-up springs open to reveal a title or caption. This pop-up is usually made of basic solid paper with text written on the top of the shape used. Pop-ups that are too intricate have a better chance of being ruined.

Standard pop-up in a scrapbook

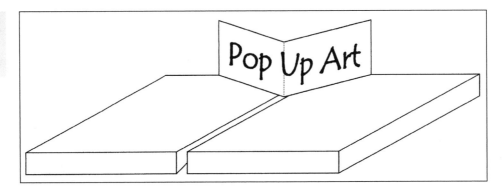

This form of pop-up is at a very high risk of coming undone. Unless it is properly put together by the scrapbooker, they are likely to come apart quickly. Every time the page is opened it will be put to work, and the more wear it gets the more it weakens. Because of this possibility, it is important that you think about how often the album will be opened.

Pop Style

Premade pop-ups are of course the easiest to use. They come ready-made with instructions that are easy to follow. You will need adhesive and decoration materials for this kind of pop-up art.

Many pop-up companies offer blank pop-ups to allow you to decorate in a manner fitting to your designed layout. If you do design your own pop-up using precut materials, be sure not to venture too far over the top of the pop-up, particularly if you are adding elaborate text. Depending on the size and style of the pop-up, they are often engineered to only handle materials on the allotted space and not above.

Because of the nature of the pop-up, it doesn't work very well in a three-ring binder. It has been tried, and sometimes works with care and precision, but the materials are less steady due to the large gap in between the pages. The best styles of albums to use for pop-ups include book-bound, post-bound, and strap-hinge albums.

The angle at which you adhere a prefabricated pop-up will determine how high it will pop up on a page. Fasten the edges of the pop-up towards the middle of each page for a wider look, or secure the ends more towards the inner edge of each page for a higher effect. Be sure to take into account how the pop-up will close with your desired height effect before you use permanent adhesives on the materials. A pop-up that is too high or wide might not close correctly.

Pop-ups that are fastened underneath the top of the scrapbook page and are made to "flip" above the page when opened are prone to ungluing and damage. These will often come undone where they were intended to be glued down, or they can easily catch on something while people are viewing the album. Consider using a style that pops up instead of flips out.

You can also create the pop-up effect on your own. You will need heavy card stock, a ruler, pencil, and sharp scissors for the initial pop-up creation. The design and instructions below are for a 12" × 12" scrapbook album. If you want to use a smaller album, adjust the size using the same proportions.

Easy Pop-Up Directions

Pop-Up
Directions

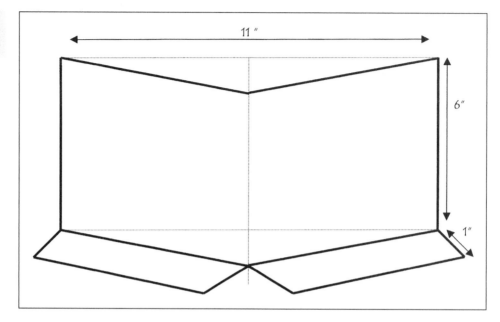

Directions for homemade pop-up technique:

1. Using a pencil and ruler, draw a pattern onto a piece of heavy card stock.
2. In light pencil, draw a rectangle 11 inches wide and 6 inches deep.
3. Draw a line down the middle of the rectangle, extending past the bottom 2 inches.
4. On the middle line, mark 1.5 inches below the top and bottom lines.
5. Use your ruler and pencil to draw a "V" from the middle marks to each corner.
6. Erase the extra lines from the original rectangle. You should be left with a wide "V."
7. Draw parallel lines one inch from the bottom.
8. Connect these lines to the bottom point (see example).
9. The end result will look somewhat like the bottom of a "W."
10. Cut out the shape.
11. Fold bottom flaps backward. Adhesive will eventually be placed on the bottom of these.

12. Simulate the pop-up method in your layout and mark where you would like to place the pop-up.
13. Decorate the pop-up with a title, figure, or other embellishments.
14. Adhere to the scrapbook page.

Pop Alternatives

Another style of pop-up is to create one inside a card within the page. The card is opened and presto, you have a pop-up! People who create and send their own cards frequently make their own pop-ups, but you can also easily incorporate them in your scrapbook layout. Card pop-ups are a more detailed form of the craft and can be made easier with the use of a brass template and folding knife.

SSENTIALS

The brand POP-Ups, by Place Class, provides designs that are simple enough for a beginner as well as excellent instructions for first-time users. Instructions can be found at ✑*www.imacrs.com/popup.htm*. Another site for excellent pop-up card instructions that can be made using the aid of a computer is with PCCreateIt, at ✑*www.pccreateit.com/popupcards.html*.

An American Quilt

Quilting is one of the most intimidating forms of scrapbooking art, but it truly creates one of the most visually appealing outcomes. Scrapbook quilts are not difficult, and with a little effort they can be fun to make. Scrapbook quilting is also a favorite subject taught at local scrapbooking stores.

Using quilting patterns that are found on actual quilts is highly recommended in scrapbooking. Many of these patterns can be found on the Internet or in the library, where there is usually a section devoted to quilting basics and its history. It is important to understand the use of color. Many actual quilters use the color wheel to assist in the creation of their quilting design.

It is very important to learn about the shapes associated with quilting. First, there are the overall shapes in a quilt pattern. These sometimes

Scrapbook
quilting

have specific names, such as the Ohio Star, or basic identifications such as a hexagon, pinwheel, flower, tumbling blocks, hearts, and circle quilts. Then there are the shapes that make up the overall image on the layout. These include basic shapes such as squares, triangles, and rectangles.

Some companies will provide peel-and-stick basic shapes for you to stick into your quilt pattern. These can be helpful, but they may not quite match the colors that you had originally chosen for the quilt. It is usually easier and more satisfying to cut a piece of patterned paper in the design you desire instead of relying on prefabricated materials.

Be aware that you might hear some "rights and wrongs" about how to go about scrapbook quilting. While there are suggestions for assisting the creation of your quilt page, there is no true right or wrong in the art of scrapbook quilting.

Photo Books

Chances are good that there will be many times when you only want to use one two-page layout in your album to depict an event or memory, but you have a number of good photos. You might be able to weed out a few pictures that are blurry or were taken from too far away and still find yourself with too many photos to fit on one page. Photo books are an excellent alternative. One photo book can fit as many as six photos.

One of the obstacles to using a photo book in your layout is the protective sleeve you use on most scrapbook pages. One option is to do away with the protective sleeve altogether for this page. Another is to carefully cut out a portion of the sleeve with an Exacto knife to allow for the photobook to come through. If you do take this step, slide a cutting mat in the sleeve and mark where the photobook will need to be exposed. Lay all of the materials on a flat surface, and be sure to apply pressure when cutting for a clean incision.

Accordion Books

One style of photo-book is an accordion book. As you lift this design, topped with your favorite photo of the subject, the remainder of the photos will emerge in a zig-zag or accordion fashion. It is very important that you use heavy card stock with this to ensure the integrity of the accordion presentation. The size of paper you will need will depend on the size of the pictures and the style in which you crop them.

Creating an accordion-style picture book in the layout

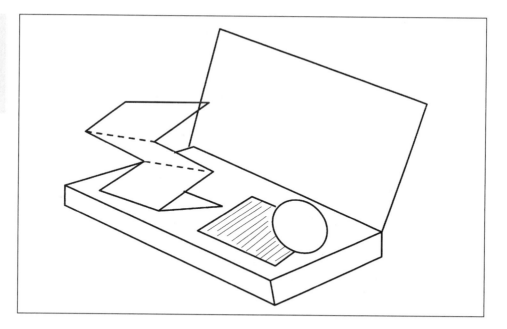

In general, you will need two pages of heavy card stock in a color that will complement the layout. Lay your pictures along one edge of the paper length to determine how wide you will need to cut. Once you determine the paper width, begin to fold the paper back and forth at that width to accommodate your biggest pictures. Other pictures that are very small can be embellished with stickers, punches, or die-cuts to fill up the space. Join two pieces of paper together to continue the flow, and adhere the end to the scrapbook page.

Ribbon-Bound Books

Another way to use photo books in your layout is create an actual book. The cover can be your favorite picture, or you can create a book cover to act as the title for the scrapbook page itself. This is a great way to save room if you also need space for memorabilia.

Be careful not to use more than six pictures in a picture book in your layout. Any more than that might threaten the integrity of the book and page because of the uneven weight distribution.

Some of the nicest bindings for books like these are ribbon or silky craft rope, much like you would see in a wedding program. Again, it is important to use heavy card stock for the pages. The limit for this style is four pages (two folded papers) that will allow room for six pictures. The bottom will be affixed to the scrapbook page and the top will be your book cover.

Flippable Frames

As a scrapbooking enthusiast, you might find two different meanings in the term "flippable frame." The first is an artistic creation in a scrapbook that acts more like a book. Two pictures are held within a bound frame back to back, and the frame is decorated on both sides. One edge of the frame is bound to the scrapbook page with a string, and the layout is designed to hold the frame when flipped in both positions: front and back.

This style of flippable frame is fun for before-and-after effects. For example, you might use it for a prom page. Title the page towards the bottom "Getting Ready for Prom." Near the top of the page, above the area for the frame, place the word "before" on the top left and "after" on the top right. Your frame might depict themes like champagne glasses and music notes or use elegant paper to relate to the occasion.

To make your own flippable frame, use heavy card stock that will be able to handle use. Punch holes into your scrapbook page and thread the thin rope through the designated areas. Tie in the opposite side for assured steadiness. Consider a theme on the reverse page that will hide the string.

Within the frame, two pictures are placed back-to-back, one taken while the subject is getting ready and one take after he or she has gotten dressed for the prom. Adhere the frame to the page that will allow it to flip to the appropriate picture underneath each word. For a two-page spread, have the second page continue the colors, theme, and portray all of the other pictures from the event.

The second style of flippable frame is a prepackaged product that provides complementary themes on either side. Some companies with flippable frames on the market make over one hundred styles for you to choose from. In this case, you would also adhere the edge of the frame to the scrapbook page. The difference is that this frame remains blank inside instead of holding pictures. The pictures instead are already affixed to the scrapbook page and the frame flips to surround them where they lie on the page.

Hidden Jewels

Hidden artistic elements can be a fun addition to the scrapbook page, providing both a creative design and additional space for elements. This is a good way to hide journaling, create more room for pictures on the page, or just to add some inventiveness to the layout. As with other artistic elements in scrapbooking, page protectors do become an issue with these techniques. It is important that you understand this before starting the creation in your page.

Window on the World

Creating windows in your scrapbook can be done with any layout, but is most fun for a layout that contains an element with windows already involved. A house, car, or tree house are all great images to use in a scrapbook page, and you can easily hide pictures underneath the window areas.

To create this, the first step is to draw or use an image for the top of your scrapbook page. Once you find areas where you would like windows to be placed, cut these on three sides with an Exacto knife, and bend the fourth side to make a solid crease. This will now create the window.

Place the top sheet onto another sheet or onto the scrapbook page itself. Lightly mark through the window with a pencil the area in which the picture can be seen. Remove the top sheet, and adhere your photos, journaling, or anything else you want behind the windows. Replace the top sheet and affix together.

Pull-Outs

Another hidden element is a pull-out. This is where a card of journaling or memorabilia is hidden behind other elements of the layout, revealing only a string or paper tab for the reader to pull and so the hidden content can be viewed. Pull-outs are wonderful in cramped scrapbooking pages, but can get frustrating and become a problem if they are too complicated. Hiding pictures in pull-outs is also a tricky task as the pictures might get caught on an element of the pull. It is best to leave the pull-out for journaling, souvenirs, or other artistic embellishments.

FACTS

Appliqué is a decoration or ornament technique that is also used in needlework. One piece of material is cut and applied to another. This is a favorite artistic technique among many scrapbook-quilting enthusiasts. Traditional patterns can be found free on Web sites promoting scrapbooking, but they are a focus of many quilting Web sites and in quilt-making books.

A pull-out can be created simply by adding an extra layer of card stock underneath the scrapbook page. Create a slit in the scrapbook layout to create the "pocket" effect. Cut a journaling card slightly smaller than the size of the hidden area, and tie a string to the end using a standard office hole punch. Slide the journaling card in and allow for the string to remain on the outside. Presto! If you now want to read about the subject matter in the picture, simply pull out the card to reveal the story!

The "before" layout using pull-out and window techniques

◆ • ◆ • ◆ • ◆

The "after" layout using pull-out and window techniques

Pockets can also be created on the scrapbook page for pull-outs. A decoration can be included on the top of the pocket that relates to the theme. This is particularly fun if you surrounded the page with pictures and only have one more space to include both a die-cut and journaling. Glue the die-cut to the top of a pocket, and create a journaling card to be pulled out from the same pocket. It's a great way to keep all of the necessary elements in a scrapbook page without rearranging your cropped photos for extra room.

Paper Techniques in a Nutshell

Paper is one of the most versatile materials to use for scrapbooking. A standard piece of paper can be made to look like it has wonderful and rich qualities. Since paper is used in so many areas of the scrapbook page, it is easy to get tired of the same kinds of cropping or cutting with decorative shears. Unique paper techniques can take away the dullness.

FACTS

Paper folding, also known as Tea Bag Folding, is a paper technique in which European tea bag papers are folded into an elegant designs and interlocked to create decorative shapes. It involves patterned paper cut into squares, folded back and forth in half in diagonal and horizontal directions, and creating a three-dimensional square design.

Paper Tearing

Paper tearing can be a great look if you know how to correctly gain the appearance you are looking for. There are actually three ways to tear paper, and each of them produces different results.

The first style of paper tearing is to create a static jagged edge. This is accomplished by tearing the page away from you. It is often used for creating uneven hills and valleys.

The second way is to tear the paper towards you. This will reveal the paper's core and allow for a look that gradually illustrates a softer rough edge than if it was torn away from you. By showing the middle, or core, of the paper, it becomes a soft and earthy look, and can be used to represent edges of natural items such as trees.

The third style of tearing uses mulberry paper. Wet the paper with a cotton swab in the size you need and carefully tear the paper apart by pulling. This creates a wispy look and is fun for snowdrifts or grass.

Paper Crimping

Paper crimping is the easiest of paper techniques. This entails crumpling the paper into a ball and repeating this step a few times. You can also roll it on a table applying pressure to the top once it is in a ball shape. To then get a flat crimped look, unfold the page and lay it underneath a large and heavy book overnight. This will allow the paper to regain its flat quality and be easier to use in the scrapbook layout while still retaining the crinkled look that you want on your page.

Do not use a hair crimping iron on any type of paper! Some scrapbookers have tried to crimp decorative papers with this beauty product only to create scorched papers and a possible fire hazard.

Paper Antiquing

Paper used in heritage books often looks as if it has been with the pictures for years. This is sometimes the case, as many scrapbookers try to incorporate as many original materials in a heritage album as possible. However, if you must use modern materials, papers can also be purchased to look antique. Several styles can be found in the standard scrapbooking section of any craft store.

There are also ways you can create an older look yourself. For many methods, you simply need household items. First, you must make sure to start with the right paper. Dark, thick pages are best, even if the paper is not specifically designed to be antiqued. The best style of paper has a second, lighter color underneath in its core. Most pages will be labeled if they have a two-tone quality.

To create the look of aged paper, hold a portion of the page down with one hand. Using fine sandpaper, sand the material with even and straight strokes going in the same direction. Turn the paper and sand again in a perpendicular direction, creating a crosshatched look on the page. You can then lightly wisp the sandpaper over the entire page in random motions to add some variety.

Coarse art brushes are another alternative to sand paper, as are metal dog brushes, barbeque grill brushes, and small scraping tools. Some companies are now providing antiquing brushes for creating this artistic effect, but they are fairly new and hard to find.

Page Weaving

A page weave is a hearty background that allows for a great deal of texture and color in a page background. This artistic technique is not difficult, but does call for a great deal of attention to detail and time. Weaving a page essentially means interlacing different colors of card stock together, either for contrast or to create a textured backing. Use the color wheel to find complementary colors to create the design. The end result should feel a little like the weave of a crisscross basket.

Directions for creating a basket-weave page for a 12" × 12" page

1. With a ruler and pencil, make a 1" border on 12" × 12" sheet of paper.
2. Using the ruler as a guide, cut the paper with an Exacto knife along the marked frame.
3. This will result in an intact 12" × 12" one-inch frame.
4. Cut the remaining 11" × 11" page with sharp straight-edged scissors in half-inch strips (Color #1).
5. Lay the strips inside the frame border.
6. Cut the contrasting piece of 12" × 12" paper in ½" strips (Color #2).
7. Weave Color #2 into Color #1 by sliding a strip above the Color #1 strip, below the next, and so on.
8. Repeat this step by alternating the starting point above and below the first Color #1 strip.
9. Adhere the edges of Color #2 to the back of the frame.
10. Trim all of the edges of Color #2 that overlap on the front of the frame.

CHAPTER 14
Scrapbooking Your Heritage

We have already begun to preserve our history though scrapbooking current events in our lives, but recording the past is just as important. The longer this is put off in the family, the harder it becomes to retrieve information later. Chapter 14 will discuss the basics of genealogy research and provide examples of some different ways to construct a heritage album.

Knowing Where to Begin and End

The science of genealogy might be something that you never thought about before. Even now, you might not want to delve into the heart of discovering all of your family history, but simply want to be able to successfully record memories to correspond with the pictures you recently came across.

The trouble with this notion is that the process of constructing a heritage album may become the process of reconstructing your family's history. It probably isn't something you realize until you are too far involved, and then it is too hard to turn back. This snowball effect might catch you off guard if it is something you had not taken into account, and many scrapbookers feel a heavy stress level during their projects when this occurs.

Heritage Album

If and when the project turns from a simple heritage album to a full-blown research project, it is best that you understand the time and energy that will go into the task. You will be pleasantly surprised with the outcome—but it does take time! Hopefully you are up to the challenge and excited about put-ting all the information together. Be realistic with your goals, and be sure to give yourself enough time to com-plete all your research. Making inquiries, looking things up at the library, and surfing the Internet all take time.

Ironically, the easiest partwill actually be putting the album together!

Should you choose not to pursue an entire genealogical course but instead to produce an album of the photos you currently have in your possession, be sure to keep your focus in mind throughout the project. Stick with the basic details and interview family members with one purpose in mind. It might get very tempting to find out more about the person you discovered in the picture, but remind yourself how far you wanted to take the project and regroup with your goals in mind.

Step by Step

Finding your roots is a very difficult task, and at first it can seem frightfully overwhelming. If you take the research in steps, however, you might find it more enjoyable than you thought. The first, and most important step, is to write down all the information you already know. For instance, you probably already know at least some of the important names, places, facts, and dates involved. When these facts are all down on paper, you will probably be surprised at just how much information you do have at your immediate disposal.

You might find at a certain point that your more distant relatives are ignoring you and your requests for information. A color copy of the final product might prove an enticement. Keep this trump card tucked away until you really need to use it.

The follow-up to this step is to talk with everyone who might be a source. Find out what they know and add it to your already growing collection of family facts. Contact people you have never met and write to relatives in other countries. Stay on track and do not let up! Persistence will get you the answers you're hunting for.

Where to Look?

Once you have exhausted your sources in terms of relatives, it is time to start tackling family records. First look through old cabinets, boxes in the attic, and safety deposit boxes. Once you have searched the obvious places, check old family Bibles, a haven for important documents. Looking for documents in your own home, however, will only get you so far, and you might eventually need the assistance of public records.

Federal and state documents will have copies of birth certificates, death certificates, marriage certificates, and land ownership records readily available. Check local churches for information on religious events as well as weddings, funerals, and burials. Local libraries are also wonderful resources for records on education, property, and families in the area. The library is also a good place to find the history of the location where your ancestors once lived. Also, consider contacting adoption services that are willing to provide you with this sort of information.

The National and Regional Archives for each state is an excellent resource, as are records of the armed forces. Military records are harder to get hold of, but depending on your relationship to the person you are investigating, it might be worth a try. The most important information you can get from any of these sources is the basics: name, birthday, and relation. Once this information is obtained, all other information such as military records or dates for major events is a bonus.

ESSENTIALS

Check the archives of the United States Immigration and Naturalization office for interesting details on the first members of your family to arrive to the United States. Their names, dates of arrival to the United States, name of the ships they traveled on, the ports they entered, and their dates of naturalization can all be found in these records.

If you are really at a standstill, try tracing the origin of your last name. This will lead you to the countries where it originated, and if you can get through issues such as spelling and pronunciation, you might be able to get it to a very specific location. This process will bring you a whole new world of places to search, with local churches and libraries always willing to lend a helping hand.

The Resource Gallery

Genealogical and historical societies are an important place to look for heritage information. They will help everyone, no matter how much or little information you currently have on the subject. It might be easier, however, to use these resources after you have already obtained some information. They have millions of records. The more data you can provide for them, the better the outcome.

ESSENTIALS Designing a family tree is the best time to get children involved in the craft of scrapbooking. They will be able to assist with artistic elements while also learning a valuable lesson on family heritage. Consider creating a page for them to include their own version of the family tree, or allow them to start their own scrapbook through the process.

Hundreds of books are devoted to describing how you can find some sort of information on genealogy. They are filled with lists of organizations, contact information for governmental archives, and tips for finding your roots. Look for books that are devoted to giving assistance in finding records in other countries or by ethnicity; many searches will lead in this direction. Also, try to purchase comprehensive books on genealogy instead of a few specific resources. To keep an entire library stocked full of these books would definitely affect your pocketbook.

A Family Tree

Using a family tree as the opening to a heritage album

Creating a family tree is a great way to start a heritage album. Besides providing vital information, you can also make it a wonderful artistic element using techniques such as paper tearing, punch art, chalking, and any other creative element. A full family tree will not fit on one page, and you might consider using the "tree" symbol to represent the first level of the family only. A pedigree chart can them be used to extend the family on subsequent pages.

The Written History

Journaling in the heritage album begins with the gathering of information. You can provide basic information such as name, date, and relation under each picture. What can make an album special are anecdotes and stories passed down orally through the years. To begin, start questioning younger relatives. They might give insight about which older relatives told certain stories. For example, you might question a cousin who will tell you that Grandpop once told her the story of a boxing match he fought. This would then enable you to approach him with more specific questions that might put him at ease.

FACTS

In their archives in Salt Lake City, Utah, the library of the Church of Jesus Christ of Latter-day Saints, also known as the LDS Church, has millions of records of family history information dating back to the year 1538. It is said to contain the largest amount of genealogical. Visit *www.lds.org* for more information.

The Interrogation Room

Genealogical research books include lists of questions that you can ask elderly relatives to jog their memory. This type of inquiry is fine, but try not to get too caught up in the questions provided. Use them to start a conversation, but be sure to allow the discussion to take its own natural course. Too often the mistake is made to get the answers to a list of questions, and the interviewer forgets to follow up when an elderly relative opens the door to a brand-new subject.

These subjects should be accounted for in a heritage interview:

Careers: first job, companies, promotions, elected office, retirement.
Children/Family: personalities, childhood friends, milestones, sports.
Courtship: boyfriends/girlfriends, engagements, first date, wedding proposals.
Education: schools, colleges, stories, classmates, teachers, projects.
Family: pets, cars, reunions, hobbies, heirlooms, collections, overcoming the odds, proud moments.
Health: illness, accidents, statistics.

Holidays: traditions, food preparation, guests, presents, religion.

Homes: neighborhoods, street names, neighbors, corner stores, style of house, shared bedrooms.

Military: service, war.

Relatives: immediate, distant, stories, adoption.

Secrets: hush-hush family stories that might not be as embarrassing in today's society.

Special events: weddings, births, religious milestones, graduations, funerals, honeymoon.

Traditions: recipes, night routines, special family moments.

Vacations: travel stories, locations.

Snail Mail Versus the Internet

There are two primary ways to interview relatives. The most efficient way is to write a letter or e-mail that includes a survey. The letter should include a description of why you are trying to put the information together. Encourage them to fill out the enclosed survey, and include a self-addressed stamped envelope. The second way is to tap into the immense popularity of e-mail. This can prompt fast results, but the style of writing in e-mail compared to a letter is very different. E-mail is quick and easy, but a letter captures a story in handwriting that can be included in the scrapbook. Consider sending the survey on acid-free paper as a means of collecting more than just stories for future generations.

Be careful not to stick a microphone in the face of an elderly ancestor! The thought of being recorded might intimidate them. Consider using a tape recorder with a hidden microphone that you can place by your side. Use a long tape and try to stay away from digital recorders that only record for a short period of time.

The most up-and-coming way to gather family information is to create a family Web site devoted to finding out information on the heritage of your ancestors. If you are very tech-savvy, why not use the Internet to help your interviews? The Internet survey results can be downloaded into a database where you will be capable of searching for information by each question, year, person, and so on. If you are looking for fast information and have the technological know-how, this is one of your best bets.

The Heritage Album

After you have acquired all of the necessary information, creating the actual heritage album will seem like the easy part! The first question you need to decide what audience the album is geared towards. By figuring this out, you will be able to figure out how to address each person in the book. Every person has many labels, and you might have to choose between names like Nana, Great-Grandmother, or Mother for the same picture. This label will depend on whom you give the book to. For consistency, you might try using the ancestor's proper name throughout.

Person, Place, or Thing

The style in which you organize the book has a lot to do with the materials you put into it. There are three primary methods of album organization: chronological, person, and subject. For pictures in which you know little more than the name and approximate dates, a chronological album is probably best. This will allow you to give a little order to an otherwise disorganized system.

FACTS

The Web site ✑ *www.ancestry.com* allows users free access to the Social Security Administration's database of people who have passed away. It is a great tool if you would like to pinpoint exact dates of death provided to the government agency. Users need the social security number of the person whose information they are requesting. They have over 66.6 million records and are updating the database regularly.

Another way to organize the album is by person. Group the pictures together and have the album cut into sections, with one ancestor being the focus of each section. It can then be organized by date. You can follow each person through his or her life, but for the most part your scrapbook will permit the reader to get to know the personalities of each person by focusing a large section on them. It will also help journaling. You can devote large sections of each page, or separate pages all together, to storytelling about this particular person.

Using a school photo in a heritage album

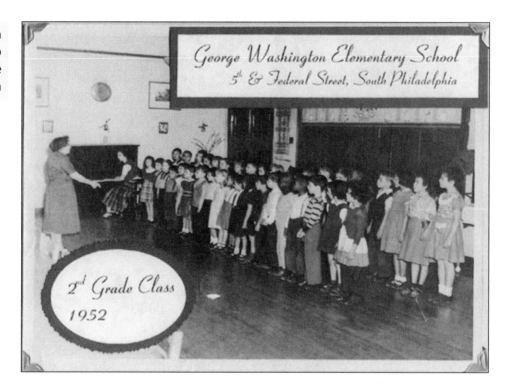

Finally, breaking the book down by subject might be a good alternative if you have groups of pictures from major events. It may be that the only photos that have been saved are wedding photos, school photos, or other important milestones in the lives of a family. If this is the case, sectioning the book by subject will encourage you to journal about why these circumstances were so important to the heritage of your family.

Why, Scarlet!

The colors that you use in the scrapbook album should reflect the theme of heritage. The primary color you might find that resembles an old-time look is shades of brown. This is a color that you should use, but try not to get caught up in using too much of it! You can use many different color combinations and modify standard colors to give the same look.

Are you the rightful owner of the pictures you intend to use in the heritage page? When you are going through the old photos found in an attic, think about cousins or other distant relatives who might be a closer relation to the ancestors in the pictures. Consider making copies of these photos if they are essential to the outcome of the heritage album.

One of the best ways to signify heritage is to use one dark muted color along with its counterpart in a brushed pastel. Usually these two shades would not be used together, but in a heritage album they represent the pictures well. The dark color should be more predominant, allowing for its brushed pastel counterpart to back photos, shadow lettering, or be mounted with journaling.

The colors navy and mauve are common heritage colors, and these look particularly good when used with the paper roughing technique. Other colors include many from the brown family such as beige, light brown, and cream. Black is a widespread complement used in antique albums. It is best to use when applying a gold or silver gel pen to the page for lettering or journaling. All in all, be sure to keep the colors flat for a successful heritage-looking layout page.

Antique Embellishments

There are a number of other elements that will help to antique a page. Materials such as lace or mesh, fashionable in previous decades, will automatically bring the page back in time. Instead of using a real piece of lace, a lace effect can also be achieved using paper and a decorative border punch.

Using embellishments to provide an antique look

VINCENT & CARMELLA DEFRANCESCO

Using buttons on your page will provide the old-time look while also outfitting the album with some dimenions that complement through texture. Glue old flat buttons around a frame, or better yet, on the four corners of the frame to add some balance. Fasten one to the page over a small piece of mesh and tie through it a small satin ribbon. To show movement on the page, place a button near one corner of each picture and use a thin piece of old-fashioned ribbon to flow through each button across the spread.

Words can assist in bringing a page back in time, and you might think about using poetry or sayings that express family heritage, pride, or history. Noting the events of the time, using famous quotes, historical data, or significant discoveries will help the reader determine the era. For example, if you are recording a page on your great-grandmother from the 1930s, you could use statistics of the Great Depression, presidential races, or anything else you can find out about the setting that would be of interest, such as music or movies. You might also consider the objects of the time and include die-cuts or drawings of old-time cars, sweeping hats, or lace-up boots just to name a few.

The Autobiography

You now understand the importance of family preservation and journaling to allow future generations to understand the family dynamic. This does not, however, stop with you. It is very important that you try to record your own life stories and hopefully promote the same kind of historical recording in years to come.

ESSENTIALS

There are a number of Web sites devoted to genealogy. To get you started, try the following Internet sites: ✍ *www.genealogy.com,* ✍ *www.ancestry.com,* ✍ *www.genealogytoolbox.com,* ✍ *www.globalgenealogy.com,* ✍ *www.heritagequest.com,* ✍ *www.ngsgenealogy.com,* and ✍ *www.familytreemaker.com.*

The easiest way to begin an autobiography is to answer the same questions you asked all of your relatives. Go through each one and detail them in a journal. Once this is complete, use the same journal to record life stories as they occur. Keep this by your bed and jot down notes each night.

FACTS

The Census Bureau is a wealth of information on family heritage. Details including name, age, occupation, and birthplace can be found from 1790. This source is better for earlier information, as The Privacy Act of 1974 restrains anyone from gaining personal data from the Census Bureau if the information is less than seventy-two years old. Check out ✍ *www.census.gov* for more details.

Another way to have an autobiographical story is to include it in the heritage album. This works best if you break the album down in chronological order. Make sure that you are included on one of the last pages, and allow for two or three pages following your pictures to be "your" story. Remembering yourself is very important. Many scrapbookers create heritage albums of their parents and of children—forgetting about themselves altogether. Creating a mini-autobiography will change this aspect and might help to jumpstart a new hobby of personal journaling.

CHAPTER 15

To the Ones We Love

Most scrapbooking enthusiasts will tell you that they originally discovered the craft when deciding to put together an album of their children, friends, or family. Preserving the memories of our loved ones is the highest priority, and capturing all of the fun and important moments in our lives with the people we most care about is at the heart of scrapbooking.

Baby Be Mine

No matter how exhausting parenting is, many mothers find some time to create a baby book. This might be as simple as recording significant dates of events or as complicated as a very detailed journal and photo book cataloguing the first days of a child's life. A baby scrapbook falls somewhere in between these two extremes by providing both pictures and journaling stories within the album.

Birthing Basics

The first page of a baby book can be most poignant when it is a simple layout. Start the album with a poem signifying a birth, or with a 5" × 7" picture and the baby's statistics including name, birthdate, birth time, weight, and height. It is sometimes best to make the colors of the first page reflect the sex of the baby. Even though you see that your baby is a girl or boy immediately, chances are that others would need to guess, especially from pictures taken in the first days of his or her life. Using shades of blue for a boy and pink for a girl will help to represent the baby.

You might not get the pictures you had intended with your labor and delivery! While some pictures of this event would be nice, even the most devoted scrapbooker might have her camera ready only to throw it across the room when the time actually comes.

While many women now keep a pregnancy scrapbook detailing events of labor and delivery, the birth story is a significant and important part of a baby scrapbook as well. Your child will cherish an itemized account of the events leading up to the birth in years to come. Labor and delivery stories are often so rich with detail that the story will add enough color that photos are not needed. Make sure you detail even the less significant items because the things that might seem annoying or silly now will probably be the elements that your family will laugh at later.

A birth story
layout

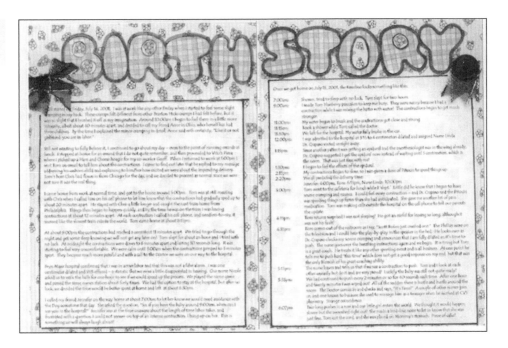

Delight in the Details

For both chronological baby albums and others, try to take a picture of everyone at the hospital that visits with you. In a two-day period, which is the average childbirth hospital stay, you will hopefully not get so many visitors that taking their picture with the baby would be overwhelming. These pictures of loved ones holding the new baby could be made to fit on one two-page spread with the caption "I am so loved!" or "Who are these people?!"

One of the album pages can also be devoted to the birth announcement. This is also a great place to fit a baby hospital picture. Try not to include much more on this page, as these are two important pieces of memories for the baby and you might want to save other items for future pages. Do include journaling on how the baby reacted to the camera in the hospital, how the baby fared with the hospital staff, and how many birth announcements you sent out.

It is also important to include a page devoted to the daddy. While he may be in many of the pictures taken at the hospital, there is little that is directed to him with the birth. A layout that shows his tender moments with the baby, affectionate moments with the mother, and journaling that tells his side of the story are important to include. You might also think about certain quotes he had during labor and delivery or nervous comments he made to others.

Baby Bonnets and More

The gifts you receive after the baby is born are always appreciated. One idea is to have a "gifts" page of the scrapbook devoted to showing off some of these beloved items. Over a two-page spread, have some pictures of the clothes, blankets, or other items that you cherished. Make a journal entry for the baby to explain all of the generosity. Since you cannot take a picture of every gift, make a list and put it into a small envelope that can be fastened to the layout. The child will appreciate this in future years.

Fabulous Firsts

Baby's first bath layout

A baby book will usually capture the first twelve months of life. Many scrapbooks will have a two-page layout devoted to each month. It is fun to start or end this section with one page that has a montage of pictures carefully placed by monthly birthday. Showing the immense changes in the baby from month to month often turns out to be one of the favorite pages in a baby album.

Other pages include recording many of a child's "firsts." The first twelve months are so full of significant accomplishments that it is often difficult to remember them all— particularly when you are running after the baby in the later stages of the first year.

First twelve
months
layout

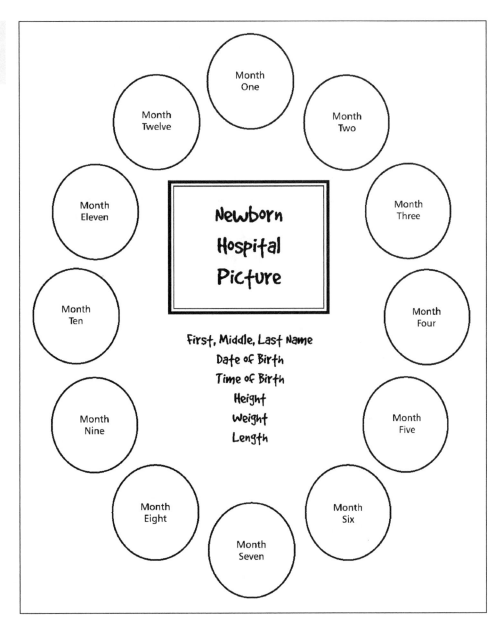

Growing Up Too Fast

The first year of a child's development goes by so fast, and before you
know it you have a toddler, grade-schooler, and then a teenager running

around the house. Remembering the events and milestones that take place during these years is just as important as documenting his or her infant year. There is probably no need to create a scrapbook each year as you might have done for the baby book, but an album that does record some of their growing up will be cherished by your children when they themselves are grown.

ESSENTIALS

Is your child scared of the dark? Combat this by taking pictures of the hiding places where creatures are supposedly concealed. Create a scrapbook page titled "There Are No Monsters in My Room!" with pictures showing the room free and clear of evil doers. Every time your child gets scared, you can now flip to this page and remind him that he is safe.

Milestones and Memories

Friendship page layout

When deciding on the page layouts to put together in the album, think about all of the memories you have from when you were a child. Which of those memories would you have liked recorded in an album yourself? By the same token, there are probably things you do not remember from your childhood because they were never recorded. Consider this factor when creating a memory book for your child.

The first step, and perhaps the most important, is to capture the most significant milestones in your child's life. These include early landmark events such as the first day of school, losing a first tooth, or sleeping in a "big bed" to later events like the first day of high school or senior prom.

When creating the style and layout for these pages, keep in mind that you did not experience them firsthand. Ask your son or daughter about the day for journaling purposes, and pull out details that they might brush off as embarrassing or unimportant.

Pages depicting childhood friends are very important in the scrapbook as well. So often we lose touch with our friends from early years, only to wonder later what happened to them. Sometimes it is too late and we do not have any way to get in touch. Prevent this from happening to your children by creating pages detailing the facts about particular childhood friends. Record their addresses and telephone numbers, parent's names, and any other details that will help your child find any long-lost friends in the future.

Hobbies and Sports

Sports page layout

Favorite hobbies and sports might have their own album! There will be so many newspaper clippings, music recital programs, and other bulky materials that you might find it easier to create a new album altogether. When creating these books, write down quotes and comments from your child. This will help them see the album from their point of view. Journaling in the album from a spectator's point of view, such as your own, will detail the events from a different angle altogether. For example, your perception of your son's football touchdown reception might be very different from his viewpoint. This is how a journalized scrapbook page might look from two different points of view:

Mother:

It was a perfect touchdown reception. Frank caught the pass with ease and ran past many bigger boys with a great deal of speed toward the end zone before dramatically diving for the touchdown.

Son:

The ball wasn't even meant for me and the coach later reminded me that I ran the wrong pattern. I cut off my teammate and caught the pass meant for him. The defense got so confused that I was able to get ten yards ahead of them before they realized what had happened. I got caught from behind and tackled into the end zone.

The Little Things

The small things that make your children unique with their own personalities often get passed over in a scrapbook. Documenting details such as favorite sayings, sleeping positions, favorite toys, and even favorite foods can be a cherished gift. With food, for example, it might seem a little odd, but the changes of likes and dislikes that a child goes through with food are often amazingly extensive.

ESSENTIALS

Moments like a twelve-year-old dancing at a wedding, a broken arm from a fall, or even reasons why your child is scared of the dark can all provide memorable pages for the scrapbook. If you remember that the book is one day intended for their enjoyment, the chances are that they will appreciate being reminded of these events in years to come.

Make some notes of their favorite foods and take pictures of the table before dinner on a few nights. On a two-page layout, record all of the serious dislikes they claim to have, and journal about times when they refused to eat dinner. They will get a charge out of their childhood eating habits in years to come, and they probably will find it amusing that the foods they used to hate they now adore.

Another cute page is to portray some awkward moments and growing pains in a child's life. On the surface it seems like a cruel punishment, but these are milestones just the same. Specific events like a first date or school dances are obvious moments to capture.

Family Reunions

Family reunions are some of the best unscripted events to capture in a scrapbook. Go to these events with some layout pages in mind, and chances are you will come back with wonderful pictures to go along with them! If you are scrapbooking pictures from a previous event that you may or may not have attended yourself, try to talk with some of the relatives that were in attendance to get a better idea of family reactions and stories.

Arranging the Album

One of the first pages in reunion albums can be a full picture of everyone in attendance. This can simply be topped with the family name and date of the event. Save the details of journaling for other pages inside the album. Use a classical look in perhaps a heritage-page style to capture the timeless elegance of the family.

SSENTIALS

Quilt pages are excellent to use for a layout of a family reunion. They provide ample room for many faces to be placed into one format. Consider using a quilt page for different generations, all of the children in attendance, or to highlight a particular portion of the family.

Subsequent pages might consist of photos and stories of groupings of people. Pages for certain generations, sisters, cousins, aunts and uncles, grandchildren, and great-grandchildren are some examples of how these pages could be organized. How you name these pages will depend on whom the book is being designed for. An "Aunts" picture to you might be a "Sisters" picture to your mother. As with heritage albums, these names are a significant part of the album and should be considered from the get-go.

Sit Back and Observe

Be sure to capture as many stories as you can from the actual reunion, but also keep in mind that you might learn new stories about the family's past or roots. These are perfect for a heritage album or to include as facts throughout the reunion album. Learn about family legends, talk with family members you might never get to see otherwise, and keep a journal with you to jot down notes. This is the time to gain family facts. Bring a list of items you might not be able to find on your own, and spend a little time with various family members talking about your questions.

Circle of Friends

Friendship albums are put together as gifts when significant milestones arise, such as a particular birthday, or when a major event is occurring to one member of the circle of friends. The one standard concept for friendship albums is to answer the five "W" questions in the opening pages of the book. This is a little different than other theme albums, but these answers are not as obvious as an album created for a family member of other special event.

QUESTIONS?

Should I date the friendship album?
Yes! It is important to date all scrapbook albums, especially the friendship album. This will show the reader how many years of the friendship will be illustrated in the keepsake book.

Who

Begin with who is in your circle of friends. This page will detail the names of everyone in the group. It could include one group picture of the crowd, or individual pictures of everyone around the page. The page might also show where everyone is originally from to indicate the range of the group. A circle of friends from college might have a very diverse background, while a group from high school would probably be from the same area of town. In this case, using street names and house numbers would be appropriate.

What

The next page answers the question "What brought you together?" Sometimes this is not as easy to answer, particularly if the friendships were built over a long period of time. For the most part, however, you will be able to figure out something poignant that truly captures the event that brought you together. Think about the sports you played, the activities you shared at college, or the significant time in your life that was the catapult to your friendship. The title of this page will reflect whatever it was that brought you together, such as "The Fall 1991 Pledge Class" or "Seventh Grade Lacrosse Team." If you do not have any pictures depicting the events that brought you together, consider a page of reflection where you can describe the events through journaling.

Where

The next question, "Where did you meet?" might be answered in part on the page devoted to what brought you together. This page could be devoted to specifics such as school names, college dorms, sorority house locations, or neighborhood streets. If you met at work, backtrack to take a picture of the location and devote your page to facts about the environment. A page for next-door neighbors might have a picture of the two homes and the street sign surrounded by memories of growing up in the neighborhood together.

When

The time that you met will have a big influence on the types of items that are in the book. Try to pinpoint the date that you met, or answer "When did you meet?" with as much precision as you can muster such as "First week of college, September 1990." This page might also depict other significant world events that took place as your friendship began.

Why

Finally, the most important question to answer is "Why did your friendship last. Choosing our friends is one area of our lives where we have complete control. As your friendships blossomed, you wanted them to succeed. This page can be silly by including pictures from some of the same likes and dislikes, "We both love a Dairy Queen Blizzard" or "We can't get enough shopping!" It should also include touching elements explaining to your friends just how much they mean to you and why you are so proud and honored to have them as friends.

Our Furry Friends

Example page of a pet album

One of the most special books devoted to a loved one is a pet album. Often thought of as a son or daughter, your pet is as much a part of the family as anyone else. Devote a book to the pet from the moment you found her to the present day. The opening page might be similar to a baby book, signifying little information besides a portrait picture and the statistics of acquisition. This is also a good place to detail a pedigree in purebred dogs or other facts like previous owners.

The Fashion Shoot

Pet pictures can sometimes all look the same, so try to be a little inventive to combat this tendency. Use different backgrounds for your pictures, and try to capture the pets doing different things, such as sleeping, running, playing with a baby, in a playground, or anything else that would be different from the previous picture. It is also important to purchase a special pen to remove red-eye from your pet pictures.

Pets are People Too!

As with a baby, use the album to record the milestones of a pet. The loss of a first tooth and becoming fully housebroken are important landmarks. Other significant moments are times when the pet might do something noble and worthy, such as protect a child in the family, visit a nursing home (with you of course), or make friends with other local pets. We are often so proud of our pets and love to talk about the good things they have done; why not record these in a pet memory album?

Beware of flash photography with your pets. They are not aware that a flash is forthcoming and are often startled by the bright light. To prevent any anxiety this could cause, including fear of the camera, consider taking pictures of your pet outside and avoiding the flash altogether.

The Church Family

For many people, places of worship provide an extended family that they depend on for support, guidance, and company. They are the places we have most of our significant experiences, including weddings, funerals, and religious milestones like baptisms, holy communions, and bat/bar mitzvahs.

A religious album should start with pages depicting the neighborhood and location of the church or synagogue. Take pictures of the outside and inside to remind you years from now of how it looks at the time. Mention the dates that family occasions took place in the church, and journal about how the church was decorated and who attended these events.

Remembering the people involved with the church is most significant. If you can, take pictures of the religious leaders and talk with them about times that they remember you and your family in the church. This will help you to journal from a perspective other than your own. Try to keep memories of other families that you frequently spent time with in the church, or members who made significant contributions of time, song, and music.

Also record a year's worth of events that you attended. Since most local religious organizations depend on yearly affairs to raise some money, they usually run in a cycle that is repeated annually. Chances are you have attended more than one yearly event. Try to have some patience with the length of time it will take you to get pictures from affairs in all of the seasons like the summer barbecue, fall spaghetti dinner, holiday party, and spring carnival. This is not to mention all of the other smaller events like bingo, classes, Sunday receptions, and so on.

ESSENTIALS

Check out the graveyard of your local church to give you a sense of changes in the congregation. You might even be surprised to find the gravestone of a family member you did not know was located at that site! The church office will usually be able to provide you with all of the facts surrounding each grave.

Additionally, your place of worship might follow traditions specific to the region you want to memorialize. Talk with everyone involved with these traditions, and get their history. If possible, visit the archives for a full appreciation of the church history and background of your church family. Make special notes of what the tradition entails, what it means, and how it changed over time. Use these facts in the album to give it an interesting flair.

CHAPTER 16

Home for the Holidays

The holidays are a time of joy, peace, and family get-togethers. They are also a time when hundreds of pictures are taken! Recording the holidays can be cumbersome, and deciding on how you want to organize your scrapbooks will take time. This chapter discusses several holidays and ideas surrounding the preservation of these memories.

It's a Holly Jolly Christmas

The Christmas album can also be used to capture memories from church, Christmas caroling, and to jot down your favorite songs. Mention in your journaling pages some family traditions—and don't assume the scrapbook viewer will know what you are referring to on the page. For example, if your family tradition is to make the Italian "Feast of the Seven Fishes" on Christmas Eve, take pictures of the dinner and record the meaning of the ritual in the scrapbook. You might even note the recipes and any meaning behind each of them.

Make sure you give Santa a hearty treat! Take pictures of your children in their nightgowns preparing a snack of milk and cookies for Santa Claus. Use this on the same layout page with a picture of them sleeping peacefully before the big morning.

While your traditions might seem obvious to you, your descendants four or five generations from now might have forgotten this family heritage altogether. A full description in a scrapbook might inspire a future generation to embark on the tradition once again.

Oh Christmas Tree, Oh Christmas Tree

The process of getting your Christmas tree is always a fun-filled family event. Stories of getting the perfect tree can make memories that will be laughed about year after year—and there is no doubt that during the current tree-buying experience comparisons will be vocalized by some family members.

Whether you purchase your tree from a chain store, from a corner stand, or cut one down in the forest, recording these events will help to remind your family members the facts about former Christmas trees. Make a scrapbook page that notes where the tree was purchased, how much it cost, and its height measurement. Be sure to include a journaling section to tell the tree-buying story.

ESSENTIALS

Do you have many stories about how and where you acquired some of your most meaningful Christmas tree ornaments? Write them down and make some scrapbook pages about these memorable items for your children and grandchildren to cherish. Take pictures of the particular ornament and include it with the journal stories for an ornament section of a holiday scrapbook.

Trimming the Christmas tree is also a tradition that should be documented in a holiday album. Every family has their own traditions for decorating the tree. Take pictures of family and friends as they place each ornament on the tree, and journal funny moments of the event. A new tree trimming tradition might even be to read through the holiday scrapbook from years past.

Holiday Cards

Example page from a "12 Days of Christmas" album

◆ ◆ ◆ ◆ ◆ ◆

Creating a scrapbook cover from used holiday cards

How many of us receive a lot of holiday cards each year without knowing what to do with them? We might not want to keep them all, but some delicate, artistic, homemade, and especially picture cards would be wonderful additions to a Holiday Card Album. Consider keeping a separate album for these cards that can be added to each year.

Holiday cards are wonderful for scrapbookers because they can help to inspire poems or sayings that might be included in future scrapbooks. They also have wonderful styles of lettering and color coordination that scrapbookers can use to help inspire layout pages. Keeping a separate card album will preserve these treasures in a safe environment while also making them easier to find than rummaging through drawers full of old letters! Be sure to use a deacidification spray to truly preserve these items.

Jewish Holidays

The Jewish holidays are rich with tradition, rituals, and color. Creating scrapbooks to represent these holidays can turn into a wonderful lesson for the children and entire family. These events are also a time when Jewish families come together and often result in many generations of one family celebrating at the same location.

QUESTIONS?

What is a Sukkah?
A Sukkah is a hut that is built to commemorate agricultural origins to celebrate Sukkot. It is constructed outdoors and can be decorated with produce and other earthly elements. The room is meant to be open to allow for the stars to shine through and rain to enter. Document the building of a Sukkah for your family scrapbook!

Most of us need to scrapbook holiday pictures piled high in our storage areas before we can consider planning to document future years. It is always difficult, however, to scrapbook previous holidays because the years begin to run together!

To create an album of Jewish holidays with pictures from previous years, try to remember the holidays by journaling notes of the activities of the day, reminiscing with photos of children dressed up for synagogue, and asking family members about specific years. Keep in mind that the most important aspect of this process is to make sure the photographs are in an acid-free environment, and as long as you take care of this need, you can begin to focus on the future. Since you now have control over documenting upcoming events, consider using the meaning of the holiday for your album and plan accordingly.

Hanukah—The Festival of Lights

One of the most important figures associated with Hanukah is the number eight. There are eight branches of the Hanukah candelabra, called the Menorah, and eight candles representing the miracle of the oil burned through eight days. The holiday itself lasts eight days, during which lessons are taught on Hanukah themes and gifts are opened. Many Hanukah scrapbooks have had the theme of "eight" throughout the album.

Consider putting together a holiday scrapbook that contains two-page spreads on how the family understands common Hanukah themes such as Tzedakah, or Charity. Focus on good deeds and other lessons that were learned through family practices, community service, or other experiences through synagogue. Use the theme of a miracle, the basis for the holiday altogether, to help determine your layouts, page designs, and titles.

There are probably many traditions that your family conducts surrounding this holiday, and scrapbooking these events will be cherished for future generations. For example, create a page showing the family children helping to set the dinner table or make latkes. Journal the method each family member gives and receives presents. Document any personal traditions you might have on one certain day of the Hanukah season. Photograph the lighting of a candle on each night or playing with the dreidel. Through it all, however, remember the spirit of the holiday to capture your layout design.

Passover

Passover is one holiday where rituals are played out in the home instead of a key place of worship. The Seder dinner takes place on the first night of Passover and is an ideal evening to document for a family scrapbook. From the traditions on the table to the interactivity among the family, a book recording these events will be appreciated in the coming generations.

Begin your Passover scrapbook or pages with photos of the family getting ready for Seder. Some of these could be pictures of food preparation or children setting the table. You might capture photos of one or more of the symbols from the seder plate being prepared, such as bitter herbs or the Haroset mixture (nuts, apples, cinnamon, wine), or preparing the dinner with pouring the wine or the cup of Elijah.

Pictures or journaling might be used to document the custom of removing Chametz from the house or placing a cushion on an armchair to symbolize freedom and the escape from Egypt. Finally, do not forget to summarize the hiding of the Afikomen, a piece of Matzoh that is hidden and retrieved at the end of the Seder in a game played by the children. As adults, your children they will be delighted to see scrapbook pages devoted to these wonderful memories!

Some holidays are not meant to be celebrated in scrapbooks. Solemn holidays that focus on forgiveness, fasting, and purification of the body and spirit might be inappropriate to snap a picture with your scrapbook in mind. Consider instead journaling a page for historical purposes about the significance of the holiday and its meaning to your family.

It is very important to remember the reason for the celebration, and to record this in your scrapbook. At every Passover Seder dinner, four questions are read and answered. Consider writing out these answers on a decorative note card and asking the children in the family to do the honors. Capture this with photos and devote a scrapbook layout to each question. The page design could include a photo of the child reading, the note card depicting the question and answer, and a section for the child to record what they have learned.

A Haunted Halloween

While Halloween is not one of the most important holidays, it is probably one of the most popular events of the year. Children love to dress up in their costumes and go from door to door to "trick or treat." It is also one of the most popular holidays for taking photos of children.

Costume Preparation

The albums that you create to remember Halloween should not only contain photos from the night itself but stories on how and why the costumes were created. Why did your son choose to be a Power Ranger or your daughter a lamb? Did you shop for the costumes, or did you make them from household items? What was the reaction of your children after they put their outfits on and looked in the mirror? Journaling these tidbits are much more interesting and amusing later on in life. These funny stories and crumbs of information are the special touch that makes modern scrapbooks important.

Evening Events

Besides recording the costume and events surrounding it, create pages to reflect traditions in your family during Halloween. Take pictures of haunted houses you helped to construct or hay rides that the children rode. Record neighborhood Halloween parties, costume contests, or Halloween marches in the street. Use movement in your layout page to reflect passing through these events, and journal throughout to capture the mood—whether it was jolly or frightful.

FACTS

Halloween is a descendent of the ancient Celtic festival Samhain, celebrated on October 31 to signify summer's end. It was during this period that Celts would dress as fairies and run from house to house begging for treats. Failure to present indulgences would result in practical jokes. This is where the parallel term for Halloween, "Beggar's Eve," comes from.

To the children, the candy is the best part of Halloween, and as such the trick-or-treat loot should be documented in the album with appropriate importance. Capture moments of children going from door to door, take pictures of kids walking around the neighborhood, and record the vast amounts of candy they received. You might even take pictures of the children separating the candy afterwards, trading sweets like baseball cards, or journal some of their comments when you tell them they are only allowed one piece per night!

The Easter Parade

Easter is an important Christian holiday that is made up of many fun celebrations and traditions. Designing scrapbook pages to reflect the styles and colors of the season makes creating these pages very enjoyable. Using pastels signifies both Easter and springtime, and embellishments with flowers, colored Easter eggs, bunny rabbits, and bonnets allows you to spend less time trying to figure out what die-cuts and colors to use and more time on the actual layout.

Easter Elements

Scrapbook page depicting Easter clothes

Easter-egg hunt pictures are priceless. To create a fun and inventive page, take a lot of pictures of the children from all angles. Once the pictures are developed, crop them so that the picture is an outline of your son or daughter in action. These pictures can then be strategically placed on the page to imitate the hunt for eggs and movement from place to place. Bunny rabbit stickers or die-cuts might also be used to help the page show balance and a directional flow.

Easter outfits are some of the cutest and most darling clothes for both little boys and girls. They look beautiful and often carry themselves like little adults when all dolled up. Use this time to capture their precious outfits and journal about the events leading up to selecting the outfits. Devote a scrapbook page to the outfit with arrows showing where each piece of the outfit came from and how they reacted to wearing formal clothes.

Easter Lessons

Teaching your children the important lessons of Easter is also something that can be accomplished through the scrapbook. As with the Christmas season, a scrapbook can be created that is devoted to experiences your family will share with Easter themes in mind. Record these experiences as lessons that your children can then read through.

Some of the scrapbook pages that act as lessons might include Easter-related holidays and events such as Palm Sunday or Lent. Have a photo of your children with palms, and journal the meaning of Palm Sunday on the same page. Lent is a period of preparation and reflection. Work with your children to give up an everyday luxury for the period of Lent and record these selfless acts in the scrapbook. Ask the children to write down what it means to them to give up an indulgence and what lessons they learned.

 SSENTIALS

Use your scrapbook to document important months such as Black History Month and Women's History Month. Teach your children about holidays commemorating others by documenting events or lessons that pay tribute to figures who are also represented with a holiday including Martin Luther King Jr. Day, President's Day, Mother's Day, Father's Day, Grandparent's Day, and Veteran's Day.

Take pictures of rehearsals for an Easter play, or journal notes about your children taking part in recreating the Stations of the Cross on Good Friday. All in all, capture the entire spirit of Easter by scrapbooking all of the events leading up to and including Easter Sunday for an overall holiday Easter album.

Love Is in the Air

Sometimes considered a secondary holiday, St. Valentine's Day often provides more memorable moments than some of the popular winter holidays! It is often filled with people celebrating in a festive and meaningful fashion, expressing their thoughts with affection and honor, and simply having a great time. This holiday might hold enough memories that you can create smaller theme albums on it alone.

Valentine's Day is for both lovers and friends. Families use it to express to one another their happiness at having them as a relative, and children use the day to share their love for their parents or guardians. Cards and memories from Valentine's Day are even sometimes more important to keep than other celebrations because the memorabilia and souvenirs often have more meaning.

When creating an album to honor memories from Valentine's Day, visit the local scrapbooking store to pick up materials that will help to decorate the pages. Purchase different patterns and shades of pink paper, die-cuts of hearts and angels, stickers relating to love, and mulberry paper in shades that relate to your theme. Vellum also has romantic features to use in Valentine's albums, and many stamp companies make intricate stamps that relate to the subject matter.

The types of items you might want to keep on Valentine's Day include business cards from restaurants or other paper items that can remind you of a romantic night with a loved one. Look for souvenirs that are not big or bulky, such as the cover of a play program or admittance ticket. If you would like to use awkward or large items, use a two-page spread where you will be able to explain the item with journaling and pictures on the opposing page. Finally, be sure to use a deacidification spray on these and other Valentine's Day materials, especially children's artwork created at school as gifts for family members.

The Kwanzaa Celebration

Kwanzaa is a relatively new African American holiday started in 1966 by Maulana Karenga to promote cultural reaffirmation. It is based on several

African harvest festivals and celebrations and on several principles of self-awareness. Long-standing traditions of Kwanzaa might just be starting in your family. This is a wonderful opportunity to record these family rituals in a family scrapbook. Use the album as an opportunity to chronicle the lessons of Kwanzaa for future generations to follow.

FACTS

According to Jessica Harris's 1995 book, *A Kwanzaa Keepsake,* "The name Kwanzaa comes from the Swahili word kwanza, meaning 'first.' The second 'a' distinguishes the African-American from the African kwanza."

When creating a scrapbook of Kwanzaa, use the symbols and themes to help design each layout. Create opportunity for the family to promote unity, self-determination, purpose, creativity, faith, collective work, and responsibility. Try to tie the topics of Kwanzaa into experiences that occur on each of the seven days of the holiday. Allow the children to journal the knowledge they gained and create the lessons on their own in the album.

Some pictures or borders you can use on a scrapbook page for Kwanzaa reflect the symbols that are used in the Kwanzaa holiday. These include die-cuts or pictures of fruit or ears of corn, gifts, and seven-branched candelabras. Other ideas for pages might include African-American poetry and folklore. Additionally, using the scrapbook as a family tradition and lesson book would not be complete without defining specific Kwanzaa terminology. Define these words to complete your Kwanzaa scrapbook:

Mkeka—Mat to display and act as foundation for Kwanzaa symbols.
Kinara—Seven-branched candelabra.
Muhindi—Ears of corn representing the number of children.
Mazao—Fruit.
Zawadi—Gifts.
Kikombe cha umoja—Unity cup.

CHAPTER 17

Travel
and Vacation

You have probably already taken rolls of film from the cities and other locations you have traveled. While capturing memories from these excursions might not be new, recording them into a scrapbook probably is something you are just starting. This chapter will offer some suggestions for travel and vacation albums as well as tips to make these wonderful memories colorful and fun.

Summer Vacation

Most children will have to go back to school in September with some sort of presentation, paper, or assignment detailing "What I did over summer vacation." This usually results in speaking or creating the assignment by explaining the most memorable experience, such as a week at the beach or other type of trip. A three-month vacation, however, should include a lot more detail than this, and creating a summer-vacation scrapbook with your children will help them remember and appreciate all of the childhood memories that occur over the lighthearted summer months.

Carefree Summer Memories

Most of the experiences your child will face could be considered insignificant. They probably include playing with children in the neighborhood and participating in sports or made up games. If you recall these from your childhood, you probably wish you could revisit that carefree time in your life (and probably even wish you could remember all the names of your friends). Who do your kids play with, and what games do the children assemble? What are the rules to these games?

Make a scrapbook page to document the businessperson in your child! Preserve memories from a lemonade stand on the corner to document their desire to make money. Keep a record of their profits, how they divided the money, and what they purchased from it.

Other common experiences include times when your children had friends sleep at your home. Document who spent the night and some of the cute or funny pranks that the kids played on you. What movies did they watch on television? What card games did they play? Where did they sleep: in a bedroom, or did they create their own tent in the living room? What were some of the fads over the summer that the friends were involved with, and what music did they listen to at all hours of the night?

Summer day camps are becoming more popular, and this is a time when you can get your children even more involved in the process. Every day when they come home, ask them to write down some notes of the day. What things did they do at camp, and what are some of their memories? Who are the new people they met and what are the names of their camp counselors? Put these pages of your children's handwriting in the scrapbook for preservation.

Those Summer Nights

Scrapbook page from summer camp album

Sleep-away camps are trickier from a scrapbooking standpoint. It is, however, a time when you can allow your children to have the responsibility of creating an album. It might just be a project that they embrace. One of the best ways to give the album a push while they are away is to create an 8.5" × 11" template album for them to take along with them.

Design a basic layout for each day that would include a title, room for a picture, and a place for journaling. Before they leave for camp, create enough pages for the number of days that they are away (Day 1, Day 2, and so on). These "days" will be your page titles. Trace in pencil where a picture would be placed, and then use a pencil to lightly create lines for journaling in a specific section of the book. Tie an acid-free pen onto a string and secure it to the album to prevent loss. Finally, give them one or two disposable cameras to take along.

If the kids are somewhat disciplined, by the end of the camp they will have completed most of the journaling of each day. This means that every section is almost done except for the photo areas where you can place pictures once they are developed. These designated photo spaces are also a good place to secure souvenirs retrieved from camp or brochures and artwork created.

If your child comes home from camp without filling in the album journaling, then use the camp's daily and weekly agenda to put the pieces together. Your end result will hopefully be a nice way to recollect these wonderful summer memories.

The Annual Outing

Many families have annual vacation spots they hit each year. There is obviously a reason that families keep going back to one place, and it is important to document this in an album as a family tradition. Usually these places are not too far away, allowing an easy family drive. As the children grow up, they often look forward to certain aspects and appreciate the recognizable elements. Having an annual spot also makes the occasional vacation that deviates from the norm much more exciting.

If you have an annual holiday spot, you might consider taking time out of your next vacation to walk through town and record some of your favorite things about the location. What restaurants does your family frequent? If you usually eat at one restaurant for breakfast, take a picture and take-home menu for the scrapbook. Record your favorite meals and mention what the children like to eat. If it is a real mom-and-pop shop and you know the owners, write down their names so the kids can return to these memories when they are grown up.

Of course, there too will be one-time-only experiences from your annual vacations. Many people try something just one time to say that they did it or to check it off the list. Make a scrapbook of these kinds of things to reminisce about both the fear and excitement you felt during the outing!

Also be sure to record your favorite things to see and do during the vacation. Write down a list of experiences such as renting bikes or strolling the boardwalk. Is there a major street in town? If so, journal about your evening walks down the street and your favorite shops. Do you have a place where you love to fish, swim, or sunbathe? If you are skiing, do you have a favorite slope? These details are very important to document for your enjoyment and also for your children.

Scrapbooking Away from Home

Traveling will mean lugging bag after bag in and out of a car, airport, or any other means of transportation. This can get very tiresome and, for the scrapbooking enthusiast who wants to take craft items on the trip, will be complicated. As you might already know from bringing supplies to crops, lugging scrapbooking materials with you to any place is somewhat difficult, even if you have an organized cropping bag. Materials are heavy, cumbersome, and can get disheveled very easily.

Forgetting to Experience the Experience

Before you take all of your materials on vacation with you, ask yourself about your reasoning. Are you truly going to crop while you are away? Have you been realistic in your plans?

FACTS

Be careful with scissors and other sharp objects if you decide to take scrapbooking supplies with you on a trip! You will not be allowed to carry these items on a plane. Call ahead to find out the airline/airport policy on checking items like this at the airport.

Sure, scrapbooking is a beloved craft, and many who are on vacation like to spend their time cropping. However, sometimes scrapbookers get so hooked on the idea of chronicling their experiences that they forget to have experiences. Try not to fall into this cycle.

Supply Alternatives

Instead of spending the time away from home scrapbooking, bring materials that will help you to document your experiences easily and quickly when you return home. Bring acid-free paper cut into 6" × 6" squares, and lightly pencil lines to guide you with journaling before you leave for the trip.

Also bring with you two acid-free journaling pens. Each night before bed, journal your experiences on these pieces of paper. They can then be mounted into your scrapbook with no need to continue journaling afterwards. This is a wonderful way to truly preserve your experiences while they are fresh in your memory.

Other supplies that can help include an extra camera battery (usually a specialty brand purchased from a camera store), disposable cameras for the children to use, color and black-and-white film, and an underwater camera if needed.

Pocket pages are wonderful tools to keep all of your memorabilia in one scrapbook album. Cut a "U" in a 12" × 12" piece of heavy card stock at the top to resemble the neck of a t-shirt. Fasten it onto a 12" × 12" scrapbook page creating a "pocket" with the opening at the top.

Zipper-style bags are also helpful in all sizes. Use a sandwich-size bag to hold all of your journaling cards and another to hold used film. The larger bags should be kept for all other memorabilia you collect throughout the trip. Bring a few of these and collect as many souvenirs as you can—remember that you do not need to focus on all of these in your scrapbook pages, but using them as a background will add a touch of color and flair. You can decide at home what can be used and discard the rest.

First in Flight

In today's society it is easier and more common to travel—and you might feel that scrapbooking all of these trips with your children might get monotonous. One way to combat this is to scrapbook your children's traveling firsts. When was their first flight on a plane? Their first train trip? The first time they were on a boat?

Other traveling firsts might be a first cruise, first bus ride, first trip to an amusement park, and so on. The beauty of this kind of album is that you can determine in advance what each page will represent. Earmark one two-page spread for the first train ride and let it be until the event actually happens. Once it does, you know how much room you need to fill in the pages, and you can collect memorabilia accordingly. This is also a great album to create as you go instead of creating it all at once because some of the traveling firsts will happen with a great deal of time in between.

Use titles that are common among these themes, such as a page with the title, "First in Flight." This uses the same phrase used by the state of North Carolina depicting the first flight in Kill Devil Hills. The page might be depicted with a die-cut or traced image of an airplane, imagery or words depicting the flight origin and destination, as well as journaling of the length of time the flight took. It is important to add elements including how your child reacted to the flights and the things that occupied their time (including crying). Airplane tickets and travel brochures are also wonderful souvenirs for this flight page.

Fifty States Album

One of the nicest travel gifts to give yourself is a scrapbook album chronicling travel through the fifty United States. This is a goal among many people who usually do not think to keep this kind of record until it is too late and many of these memories are lost. The fifty-states album will often inspire you to take new trips and explore states both near and far. It might help you turn a normally dull weekend into a spontaneous road trip!

FACTS

One of the trendiest albums to create is a Baseball Stadium Scrapbook Album. There are currently thirty Major League baseball parks and eleven new Major League parks are slated to open in the next few years. Additionally, there are fourteen ballparks used by the International League, sixteen ballparks used by the Pacific Coast League, and 162 Minor League baseball teams throughout the country in diverse geographical locations.

Page Continuity

Scrapbook page from a fifty-states album

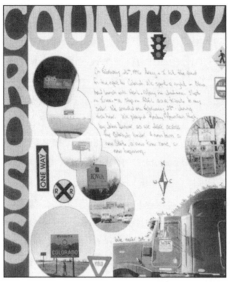

The fifty-states album is usually best done in a spiral-bound scrapbook album. These books are usually at least twenty-five pages long, allowing you to use the front and back to create your fifty pages. It is important to keep all of the states pages in one book for the best effect—which means not going overboard scrapbooking any state. It is easy to get caught up in the layout of one state, forgetting that you have another forty-nine to document! Keep in mind that a trip to another city will probably be documented in detail in a travel album, but that a fifty-state album is meant to simply highlight your trip through each of the states.

Don't forget about the District of Columbia! Use the inside of the back cover of your spiral album to allow room for what most consider the fifty-first state. Washington D.C. is such an important part of the nation, and as the United States capital, excluding it from your album would mean not capturing the essence of the fifty-states scrapbook.

A common theme will be important in this album for two primary reasons. The first is to keep the momentum going through each page. The book will need similarities and balance in the page elements to maintain its cohesiveness from Alabama to Wyoming. The second, and probably most important reason to allow a common theme to follow each page, is to make things easier on you. Using the same style of patterned paper, the same lettering technique or die-cuts, and similar forms of journaling on each page will help you to get the layouts done quickly. One of the best ways to ensure this is to purchase a bulk of the same kind of patterned paper from the beginning, ensuring you will not run out of a paper that might go out of stock.

Welcome to Pennsylvania

One of the most amusing ways to travel each state is to take pictures with the same sort of elements in every photo. This may be difficult, but if you choose standard elements then you might have fun trying to find them! For example, you could use the standard "Welcome to Arizona" types of signs, or similar signs of other cities and towns within each state. You might also try landmarks such as the Grand Canyon in Arizona, Love Statue in Philadelphia, the Washington Monument or Capitol Building, and the Golden Gate Bridge in San Francisco.

According to the Locals . . .

Traveling usually does not include any thoughts of your hometown. The world is such a busy place that it is important to slow down and take a look around. Try to appreciate the places you live and the people who surround you. Use your scrapbook to document important local traditions, locations, and historical monuments.

If you are really proud of your local scrapbook, take it to the local library to see if they want a copy! Many small town libraries will encourage you to make a color copy of your scrapbook as a way to preserve local family history.

This is also a wonderful tool for children to create with you. Let them document educational school field trips to local historical monuments and even chronicle days when they might have visited a local farm or museum with their schoolmates. Sit down together and allow them to tell you about each visit, the people they met, and the lessons they learned. Write down some of their thoughts to journal the experience and note the day and time that they visited. Also make mention of the weather to truly help them remember these educational days in years to come.

Local history is one of the best styles of scrapbooks for leaving out on the coffee table for visitors to flip through. It shows that you have a sense of pride about your hometown or the surrounding areas. It is also a wonderful tool for houseguests or family members who travel from out of town to visit. Ask them to look through the album to see if they would like to go to any of the locations, or use your guests' experiences as an excuse to get to a location you have been trying to see for some time.

CHAPTER 18
Wedding Bliss

Scrapbooking the weddings of friends and family usually takes a little more time than other types of commemorative albums. This usually corresponds to delicate care for each album page and a labor of love put into the creation of such an important heritage piece.

Wedding Album Materials

When creating a wedding album, you first need to purchase some special materials for an effective outcome. There are specialized items for wedding albums carried by all scrapbooking stores. These include featured wedding stickers, patterned paper adorned with wedding emblems, exclusive die-cuts, and related rubber stamps. Other papers used for wedding pages include simple colors of creams, whites, and metallic colors embellished with uncomplicated romantic patterns. These are most often used for mounting photos and other wedding memorabilia.

ESSENTIALS

Vellum is a common material to use when completing wedding layouts. To alleviate the problem of seeing glue through the translucent material, use a ribbon strategically placed on the ends to cover where you have used adhesive. Consider this option in advance so you know where to tie the ribbon into the overall design.

Choosing a Wedding Album

Scrapbook page from a wedding album

The wedding album itself can be created in a few different ways. The easiest but most expensive are albums especially devoted to weddings. These are usually white leather albums with gold or silver trim on the front cover. Many also have a metal plate attached to the album that can be removed for engraving. Albums in this genre range from $40 to $80, depending on the manufacturer and other supplies that are included. Many of the higher priced albums will also have wedding related embellishments to accompany the purchase.

Another way to create an album is to decorate one with materials you purchase at a fabric store. This can be done using a standard scrapbook, selected wedding fabric, thin foam, a hot-glue gun, and a sharp pair of scissors. Patterns for covering strap-hinge, post-bound, and three-ring binders can be found on many Web sites that offer free downloading. If you want to create your own pattern, do so by first using a large sheet of paper to create the pattern. Copy this pattern onto your fabric and then create the cover. Pin the fabric onto the album to ensure it fits and then use a hot glue gun for the final adhesive.

Alternate Materials

For a variety of materials not simply found in the scrapbooking aisle, a trip to a large craft store might result in interesting decorations for your layouts. National craft store chains will provide lace, tulle, and other wedding items in various sections of the store.

FACTS

Some companies provide help with the detailed task of changing your maiden name to your husband's name. The Official New Bride Name Change Kit by ✍ *www.kitbiz.com* offers a kit for the bride customized by state and zip code. For $24.95, the kit includes government forms, record change forms, directions, and a checklist. If you use this kind of kit, be sure to photocopy all of the documents for the wedding scrapbook.

You might even be able to strategically place beads to adorn particular die-cuts or silk flowers in the same color as the wedding theme. Some of the other creative materials to include are imitation certificates of marriage signed by the couple. Usually these documents will be found in the wedding aisles of any craft superstore.

The Courtship

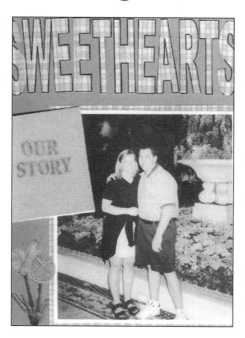

Scrapbook page depicting a courtship

A wedding scrapbook often covers the marriage ceremony and following celebration, but an effective way to create an album to truly commemorate the couple is by starting from the beginning. The courtship might have been seven weeks or seven years, and there are undoubtedly memorable moments that the couple refers to when reminiscing about falling in love. These moments usually consist of a time and place that they met, the first date, when they first met each other's family, and the first time "I love yous" were exchanged.

That Disastrous First Date

The courtship section does not have to be a very large part of the album. Figure out which days and experiences are most important to the couple. If it was the first date, take a picture of the restaurant they attended or any other means of commemorating this occasion.

Question the couple on how they felt about the other person and what their first impressions were during the date. What are some things that they really liked about each other, and what were some first impressions that have changed since getting to know each other better? Luckily most people remember the day and time of the first date, so these details should be easy to find no matter how long ago they occurred.

Every couple will be different in the types of things that stand out in their minds from the courtship period. It might simply be a romantic walk on the lake on one random Tuesday evening to something more significant like a fabulous vacation in Europe. Try to find as many souvenirs as possible from these memorable times, such as restaurant menus or travel tickets, and use them in the scrapbook.

Sweet Nothings

One art that has been lost in recent years because of the increase in technology is the love letter. These were common during courtships of years past, but with the ease of e-mail this wonderful part of dating is sometimes lost. If love letters were written to one another, place them into the book in an envelope so that they can be removed and read. You might also consider adhering the back of a trifold letter to allow it to be opened in the scrapbook but not removed. This will keep the letter from being misplaced in the future.

Use quotes from the couple to adorn your scrapbooking layouts. A title above a photo of the couple might read, "I fell in love with they way he played with my puppy. It was so cute and boyish." These types of quotes truly capture how the couple fell in love through the courtship period.

Romantic cards are most often associated with St. Valentine's Day, but sometimes they are sent to a loved one "just because." Most people keep these cards to remind them of their loved ones, and these can be used to embellish the scrapbook page. Cards that say "I love you" are also passed during other celebrations such as birthdays and winter holidays. Collect these and use them to complement photos of the courtship period.

Popping the Question

The stories behind popping the big question are usually sappy and romantic with tidbits of comic relief intertwined. The end result is a wonderful anecdote that will be told many times to friends and family as the news of the engagement circulates. This is a story that should be written down to preserve the details for descendants of the couple, and there is no better place to tell the story than a wedding scrapbook.

These engagement pages should be viewed from the beginning, and that means documenting the purchase of the ring and the decision of where and when to ask the question. If the ring is a family heirloom, record the family members to whom the ring has been passed through the years and how you came into possession of it. It might be interesting to note the style of ring, the reasons for choosing it, and any inscription that was engraved on it.

The events leading up to asking the question are something that could add detail to the layout—whatever was needed to get the plan together including restaurant reservations or hotel reservations. Most important, document how the plan was put together to keep the night a surprise. Who was in on the plan, and what last-minute catastrophes almost occurred? What kinds of fibs were told to get her to the location? Was a restaurant waiter or hotel staff depended upon to keep the plan going?

The last item to document in the scrapbook is the reaction to the question. Journal about whether or not she seemed surprised, if she cried, and exactly what she said. Also try to find out this reaction from both parties since his perception of her reaction might be completely different.

Wedding Planning

It's decision time for the details of planning a wedding, and the two of you are at odds about which wedding band to select. Back and forth the conversation runs until finally one of you gives in. Planning your wedding is meant to be a fun experience, and many of these quirky little fights are endearing and turn out to be funny stories in the end.

Planning the wedding should not take up too many pages in your album, but a few two-page spreads with titles such as "Decision Time!" or "Meat or Fish?" will be a nice transition to the actual wedding events. Since preparing the wedding takes a lot of time and is a long-term event, keep a disposable camera with you to capture some of these moments.

There are so many decisions to make, wedding halls to visit, bands to try out, and other details to nail down that there is a good chance you will forget all about bringing a camera along. Keeping one handy will allow for quick snapshots of some of these moments before you move on to the next item.

The steps the bride and groom took to make decisions about the wedding are something to keep. This might be a journal entry of when your wrote your vows, a listing of the songs selected for the ceremony and the reasons behind them, or a picture of the flowers you intend to use in the place of worship. Additionally, if you decide to marry on a beach or other alternative venue, document the thoughts surrounding this decision with some pictures from a prewedding visit.

ESSENTIALS

If your mother or other family member gives you words of encouragement while planning the wedding, write these down for a scrapbook page entitled "Words of Wisdom." These will be wonderful memories to reflect on through the years of marriage.

The wedding dress purchase is one of the biggest, and most emotional, events of wedding planning. It is the kind of thing that every little girl dreams about growing up. Capturing these moments is a wonderful way to remember the special time, and it will be a fun part of the process to share with the bridegroom after the ceremony takes place. Snap pictures of a few dresses on the bride with a title next to the chosen exclaiming, "She's the One!" or "Fit for a Princess." You might also journal the reasoning behind the choice of dress.

Bachelor and Bachelorette Parties

Most bachelor and bachelorette parties are simply an opportunity for friends to get together and celebrate the impending marriage. While these get-togethers sometimes do not have the best reputations, chances are that they are harmless enough to capture most of the event in photos.

True Sophistication

Scrapbooking a bachelorette party

One of the best ways to capture these moments is to get photos with all of the friends in attendance and spread them over two pages in the scrapbook. Underneath each picture, add insights that the person in the photo provided to the bride or groom. This should be funny instead of well intentioned, expressed with the idea that many people would be reading them in the scrapbook. When you ask everyone for advice at the party (and bring with you something to write it down), be sure to remind them to keep the comments PG-13.

Invitations and Games

Some kind of game is usually played, particularly at bachelorette parties, and documenting these in the album will also be a moment that the bride will want to remember. These diversions usually include some sort of question-and-answer session or goals that the bride will need to accomplish as the party travels to different parts of town.

Assignments like "Find someone with the same name as your first boyfriend" are fun tasks, and the results can be captured with a photograph. Top the page with the title "Labor of Love" and list the required tasks for the game. Subsequent pages can contain pictures and journaling to tell the story of accomplishing these goals.

Both bachelor and bachelorette parties are now becoming more sophisticated, sending invitations and having a predetermined agenda. As with other wedding-related events, these invitations should be included in the scrapbook album after the deacidification process. Use stickers and die-cuts such as champagne glasses, party symbols, and colorful items to decorate these pages. Also try to print out a copy of the agenda (list of bars to "party hop," games played, and so on) to complement the page.

Shower the Bride

Many brides will have at least one bridal shower, and these events are often documented in scrapbook pages along with the abundance of gifts they receive. Sometimes there is more than one bridal shower, and this coupled with a picture of each gift can get overbearing in the scrapbook. So how do you manage these events while still documenting the affair true to form? It is best to take each item step by step to create a few memorable pages.

A scrapbook layout of a bridal shower should depict some of the items that make the shower special. These include the event invitation, party favor, menu, decorations, cake, and other special items. Use as many actual items from the event as you need to help decorate the pages, and take pictures of everything else such as the decorations, wishing well, and so on.

Engulfed with Gifts

The mission of a shower is to give and receive gifts to help the couple get started in their life together. With these goals in mind, evaluating which gifts to include in the layout pages is a difficult task. It can get too overwhelming showing all of these gifts in the layout, but where do you stop? Consider taking a photo of the bride holding each gift. These photos can then be cropped to show only the gift with a few pictures portraying the bride holding the gifts. Scatter the pictures throughout the page for a montage-looking layout. It will add a unique element as well as exhibit each gift individually.

If you would rather show only a couple of gifts in the album to keep the tone of the wedding book less active, find another way to keep a record of all of the gifts received. A bridesmaid usually documents shower gifts as the event is taking place. This record acts as a guide when it is time to write thank you notes. An item such as this, created at the shower depicting all of the gifts and gift-givers, is a wonderful addition to your bridal shower layouts. Other less meaningful but related items include a printout of the gift registry, a list of invitees, or email printouts of shower planning discussions.

Scrapbook page depicting wedding shower gifts and cards

♦ · ♦ · ♦ · ♦

Wedding shower page focusing on the bride

Let the Games Begin!

Shower games are popular to help pass the time during this event and also for documenting funny quotes from the guests in attendance. These games, popularized in recent years, also offer an opportunity for brides and grooms to reveal details about their relationship as well as to be tested on how well they really know their partners.

To document the shower game in the scrapbook, you can follow the game through each question and photograph or journal key moments—particularly the points in time where the party guests giggled and expressed amusement at the answers. If possible, use the props from each shower game in the scrapbook pages as well.

The wedding rehearsal is normally held the evening before the wedding day and is followed by a dinner attended by all of the key players involved with the ceremony including the bridal party, parents and grandparents, and the wedding officiant. Use this opportunity to snap photos and document toasts for the wedding scrapbook.

The Big Event

After the prenuptial parties are finished and advice is handed down, the big day finally arrives. This should not be a time when the bride is worried about documenting details of the wedding—let everyone else do the honors. In fact, you probably should have taken care of this well in advance by finding photographers and asking friends to take pictures. After the wedding, be sure to quickly jot down notes that will help you to journal in your scrapbook when the time comes. For now, just be sure to enjoy your special day.

If this is a gift for a friend, give them decorative cards to fill out the morning after the big event. These can be white with light lines drawn to enable them to journal in a straight line. At the top of each note card, ask a question such as, "What was the funniest moment of the evening?" This will allow the couple to easily fill out the cards over breakfast or on an airplane traveling to the honeymoon. It documents the mood of the day while it is still fresh in the minds of the couple. Adding these cards to the scrapbook saves you time from journaling everything yourself while also capturing the frame of mind and handwriting of the key players involved.

Church Bells

Documenting the wedding ceremony is a special part of the scrapbook. Items that are well received on these pages include photos of the church or ceremony location, descriptions and pictures of the flowers or decorations, and photos of the guests.

Additionally, this is a great place to journal about the person who is officiating over the ceremony and to mention the history of the location in which the marriage takes place. You may have showed the location in your pages on wedding planning, but that layout should depict why you chose the location over others. This explanation might reveal its meaning to you and how it represents your love for one another.

Using a wedding program in the layout

The ceremony pages also might contain the vows written by each of you. Show what each sentence means and why it relates to your loved one. Many will use an attractive script font to add these to the album, but personal handwriting with an acid-free pen will have more meaning in the future. Additionally, poems or other ceremony readings, including those from the Bible, should be added to the layout. Using the technique of movement through a two-page spread, you will be able to design these elements to follow the order of the ceremony.

The ceremony agenda provided for guests should also be portrayed in this section of the album. There is no need for any other elements on the page besides perhaps some patterned paper or stickers to complement the booklet. Place it in the center with the back of the booklet glued to the scrapbook page using permanent adhesive.

If there is writing on the back of the program, such as a thank you note or moving address of the bride and groom, consider using a heavy string to lace into the spine of the booklet. Fasten the string ends to the page on the top and bottom, allowing you to view the entire booklet.

Dinner and Dancing

The dinner reception following a ceremony is always a fun experience to document in the scrapbook page. While many would like this to be an elegant event, the most memorable receptions are functions that are filled with dancing and animated guests. The layouts depicting the wedding ceremony will be graceful and stylish, so use the reception page designs to express a colorful and lively evening.

Professional photographers will charge you a great deal of money for additional prints of the wedding photos. To alleviate this cost, purchase disposable cameras to place on each guest table. These photos are the ones you can use for your reception layouts, and will often offer a more relaxed and spontaneous approach to capturing the evening.

These pages might also include catchy and enthusiastic titles such as "Dancing the Night Away!" Be sure to capture photos of guests enjoying themselves, smiling, laughing, and dancing. Get pictures of the DJ or wedding band and even include a song list.

According to Oxford's *A Dictionary of Superstitions,* the saying "Something old, something new, something borrowed, and something blue, and a sixpence in my shoe" can be traced back to medieval weddings. "Something old" signifies protection of a baby; "something borrowed" is lucky; "something blue" expresses faithfulness; and a "sixpence" represents the ability to ward off evil.

The reception is not only fun and games but is also usually filled with many family traditions. From the first moment of a dinner blessing or toast, these customs should be highlighted and detailed in several pages of the album. Moments such as the cutting of the wedding cake might be elaborated with text on how you smashed cake in your husband's face and planned the mischievous deed for weeks. These details will get lost through the years if you do not write them down soon after the wedding.

Honeymoon in Vegas

Documenting the honeymoon is really no different than recording memories from a special vacation, including travel plans and details throughout the trip. The nuts and bolts of the experience will be much the same as many of your other travel pages.

The differences that do show through in these pages are the intimate moments that you can document as a meaningful way of beginning your lives together. Keep a special track record of these by photographing special excursions and romantic getaways. Journal the long walks on the beach or hiking to a secluded waterfall.

 **SSENTIALS**

The last page of a wedding album is a wonderful area to journal about how much you love your partner. Use this page to thank them for being wonderful companions, loving spouses, and true friends. Formulate this as a love letter for a more creative method to express these thoughts, and add a small picture cropped in a heart of the duo on the wedding day.

Essentially, expand these travel pages from the ordinary into something special for you to enjoy and reflect on in years to come. Preserve keepsakes from these interludes together, including rose petals or romantic notes to add to the album pages.

CHAPTER 19

Specialty
Albums

There are a number of specialty scrapbooking albums that will help to define you, your interests, and your path in life. Each of these albums will be individualized toward your own principles. Use this means to document personal talents or qualities and apply these styles to your own individual life.

Home Cookin'

Every family has recipes that have been passed down through the generations. Most are learned by children watching their parents or grandparents cook on Sunday afternoons or holiday occasions, and often these recipes have never once been written down. A recipe scrapbook will act as both an opportunity to keep these treasures in one place as well as a family heirloom to be passed on through generations.

Old Family Recipes

The research style that went into creating a heritage album will also be needed to create an album of old family recipes. To get the most accurate information possible, talk with the oldest members of the family and work your way down. Ask them about favorite meals, dishes, and traditions that their parents and grandparents had during family dinners. Many of our older relatives will claim to not remember the details of these dinners, and asking them detailed questions about each meal will help to jog their memory. Some questions might include:

- How many courses were served at Sunday dinners?
- Did your mother or grandmother have a specialty that they made for guests?
- When the house smelled of food, what did it remind you of?
- What kinds of holiday cookies did your parents make?
- Was there a special dessert or pudding that you remember as a child?

ESSENTIALS

Make a handful of recipe cards to add to your scrapbook pages. Slide these behind the original recipe by creating a slim pocket with patterned paper and card stock in your layout. These will be a lot easier to give to family and friends when they look through the album and want to "borrow" it to make copies.

Many families have one kind of special holiday dinner that they make every year. These are usually dishes that are traditionally created to reflect the particular holiday, but some may simply be dinner for no other reason than to continue the custom of your family heritage. Write down these traditional meals, from the appetizers to the dessert, along with the recipes.

When the time for the dinner arrives, make special note of everyone's favorite dish as well as comments that are made about the meal. Take a picture of the table full of food with the family seated, and journal the meaning of the meal in the scrapbook page next to the photo of your family.

Whisper Down the Lane

Using family recipes in a scrapbook page

As with any oral history, recipes will change as they are passed along through the years. Once it gets to you and you try to recreate it, you might find that the result is not quite as you remember. Many times creating an exact recipe will conflict with the recipe's original style of adding ingredients "as needed." And as with all recipes, it will never taste the same as the creator's tasty dish. That being said, the recipes you document in the scrapbook page should reflect the original dish as closely as possible.

If you have tried everything and still cannot get the recipe quite right, mention this in your journaling with a related statement. For example, a family meatball recipe page might also contain the journaled text, "This meatball recipe is as close as we in the family can come to recreating Nana's wonderful dish. There is an ingredient missing that we cannot quite figure out! I guess Nana really wanted it to remain a secret!"

Personal Favorites

Recipe albums do not stop with the heritage piece. Personal favorites should be documented both for your enjoyment and for future generations to create and pass along to their children. Without a personal recipe album, your grandchildren will be trying to recreate your concoctions from memory as well! Keep this album as an ongoing project, and remember to add your recipes as they become favorites through the years.

When creating a personal recipe album, do not spend too much time on the decoration or fancy materials. Your overall design should be simple, easy, and of a style that can be picked up and recreated when you add another recipe five years down the road. An 8.5" × 11" album will be best for this kind of scrapbook and will allow you to create one to two recipes per page.

SSENTIALS Document the prices of ingredients in each recipe and date pages as you create them in the personal recipe scrapbook. This will be an amusing way to look at each recipe for future generations as they compare the cost of particular items to the current prices.

Each page in the layout should contain three major elements: a list of the ingredients, directions on how to make the recipe, and a journaling entry on when and where you often make the dish. This last element is most important if you want to maintain the "scrapbooking" element of the album and have it truly be a keepsake in the family. Keeping with this theme, the recipes and directions themselves can be done on a computer printout, but journaling the story behind the recipe in your handwriting will make the album much more meaningful.

There are also a few ways to make these pages a little more interesting than the basic three original elements. The first is to take a photo of the dish. While this is not required by any means, we would all probably agree that published cookbooks are much more effective if they have provided pictures of the dishes. It helps to give the reader a better idea of the end result, and your personal scrapbook is really not much different.

Another way that you can make the book personal is to write the directions exactly how you might say them to somebody who asked for the recipe. This will bring a distinctive element to the page that might have been lost through the generations. For example, if you begin telling someone how to make a dish by saying "First you take a pot . . . ," then this is exactly how your should begin your recipe directions.

Home Is Where the Heart Is

Many people do not think to scrapbook elements of the places that they live, but this is an important step in creating albums that reflect our lives. After all, these are the places where we sleep, eat, and enjoy time with family. Why not scrapbook this important facet of your family's history?

Scrapbooking a move into a new home

Home scrapbooks might consist of a number of places that chronicle the transition of a family through the years. For those who do move

often, it is a wonderful way to remember the good times in each location. Others might scrapbook one home that has been passed down through the generations to family members who have all created their own memories of the home.

Mr. Fix-It

While the style of the album will be very specific and unique to each family and home, the elements that are included are the same. Document all of the family members who lived in each location and their ages. Use pictures, if you have them, of the home and show each person's room and favorite element of the house. Journal about some of the major events that occurred in the home, such as weddings, babies, or first dates. Also be sure to capture little-known facts that will be treasured keepsakes like, "Patrick used to sneak to the roof and smoke!"

FACTS

Web sites can help you to document your move and the details surrounding the process of purchasing a new home. Popular sites like ✍ *www.realtor.com* offer tools such as financial calculators or "relocation wizards" that will assist you in figuring out costs and expenses. These can then be printed to keep for your scrapbook pages as a reminder of this memory.

New home construction and existing home reconstruction are also common elements to photograph for a before-and-after effect. The importance of documenting this stems not only from the need to see the differences and justify our decision-making, but to document a value on our homes.

This is commonly done through keeping materials in a file folder in the home office or desk. Putting some of these supporting documents into a scrapbook will ensure that you always know where they are held. When it is time to sell the home, simply keep the scrapbook open for potential buyers to view, or make a color copy of the album for prospective owners.

To effectively keep materials in an album that will preserve the changes you have made to the home, there are some elements that are required to be included in the layout. First, and most important, are before-and-after photos. Mount these on similar background of patterned papers. Next, include documentation on when the repair or improvement was made and its cost. If you are trying to increase the value of the home, these elements will all be necessary.

Finally, make some notes about the process that might not be included in the materials provided. This will encompass statistics on how the home is better run with the improvements in place. For example, if you replace a heating system, a potential buyer might want to know your monthly heating cost before and after the system was installed. Keep this record in your scrapbook so they have a visually appealing means of looking at this information.

A Green Thumb

The upkeep of the outside of your home and gardens will also be an important related item to document in this style of scrapbook. Not only is it one of the most beloved and cared-for elements of the home, but if you intend to sell your property in the winter months, these pages will become very handy!

ESSENTIALS

The outside of your home should not be limited to scrapbooking the flowers or shrubs. Take photos of the winter months after a beautiful snowfall to capture white snow clinging to the tree branches. Photograph smoke billowing out of the chimney or any animals that wander into your yard.

Document the kinds of trees, bushes, and flowers that surround the house, and note which elements were added recently. Jot down observations on the page about the different colors that come through, and what times of year these elements bloom. Most importantly, take pictures of the bushes or flowers in full bloom, and mat these onto the layout with the month the photo was taken underneath.

Capture each time of year by scrapbooking seasonal events, such as raking the leaves or planting bulbs. Most important, photograph and journal the way your family interacts with the outside of the home, how they use it for play, and how they care for its surroundings.

The List Album

Scrapbooking a goal in a life-list album

There are a number of resources on the market that act as motivational tools for us to create a "Life List." These are simply lists of goals you want to accomplish at some point in your life. Lifetime goals really do help to inspire every one of us to achieve a certain standard, visit different locations, and often add an element of thrill to our lives. A life list might contain some things as basic and important as "Have children" to other more unique items such as "Climb a mountain" or "Scuba-dive on the coral reef."

A scrapbook is one of the places where you will be able to display your life list. It is also a wonderful way to document each of these accomplishments. One of the best ways to start the project is to sit down and create a list titled "50 Things to Do Before I Die." This list will fit into a scrapbook if you use the front and back of each album page.

ALERT

Some of the objectives in a life list may take you a long time, and it is easy to feel like they will never be completed. Consider designing layout pages for the goals that are more easily completed to give you a sense of accomplishment. You can then fill the album slowly with some of the difficult goals to achieve as they are completed over the span of your lifetime.

Once your list is complete, purchase an album that is especially used for "The List." The pages should not be premade with decoration or layout since each experience will bring unique qualities that you may want to include in the design. Instead, lightly pencil each goal onto their designated page to keep them in the order that you wish.

Amazing Achievements

Albums that represent a significant achievement in our lives are important to create. They remind us of the hard work and effort that went into the subject, and they help us to appreciate and feel good about ourselves. These albums usually represent something that occurred over a long period of time and took determination and energy to bring to fruition.

SSENTIALS

Hobbies are personal topics that should be documented in a scrapbook. When you find something that you really love, it is easy to spend a great amount of time of your life devoted to the subject. Why not create a scrap album devoted to these pastimes?

Retirement albums are a wonderful gift to give to someone who is ending their career and starting a new era in their lives. If you begin to create a retirement album, be sure to talk with family members or others who know a great deal about the career of the person being honored. Ask coworkers to each write a little something about the retiree by providing them with acid free paper and a journaling pen. Collect these to add to pages with photos of coworkers and former places of employment.

Another personal achievement is an awareness album. This scrapbook documents and teaches one particular subject close to the family. Creating an album for topics like overcoming a serious illness or other traumatic diseases is a healing mechanism. It is also a wonderful way to commemorate those who have assisted the family in this ordeal. Additionally, creating a scrapbook with a child who is affected by the difficult circumstance will help them to learn about these complicated subjects.

Dewey Defeats Truman!

The last time you rummaged through your parent's attic you probably found yourself in awe at the way old newspapers captured the moments in time with such a wonderful expressive description. Chances are that you or someone that you love will rush to the store to get the newspaper after a newsworthy event occurs. The reason we store this memorabilia is primarily to help our grandchildren and great-grandchildren experience the event through our eyes. They will see the newspaper and understand the state of the world as these events took place.

Storage Conditions

These newspapers, however, are probably rolled up in the attic being attacked by moisture, heat, and sunlight. They are most likely yellowed, dry, and brittle. Newspaper is one of the most inexpensive types of papers, full of the material called lignin that will eventually cause its destruction. It is important to rethink how you save these kinds of materials to ensure that they will be readable for future generations.

Use a sturdy album to handle encapsulated magazines or other memorabilia that will be heavier than a normal scrapbook page layout. Keep this in mind when you decide on how many pages to have in the album as well. Quality three-ring binder albums are usually excellent with heavier materials.

Using a deacidification spray on these old articles and news events is a must. You must also keep the news album (and all other scrapbooking albums) away from moisture and heat. Since newspaper articles might be awkward or large, 12" × 12" albums are usually more fitting to their special needs, and a two-page spread will often cover only one article.

Newsworthy Scrapbooking Materials

Colors and other materials often used in scrapbooks, such as die-cuts or stickers, usually have no place in a news album. You might use some patterned papers that are complementary to the subject of the news, but for the most part many of these memories of news events are solemn and the pages should reflect this.

Whatever circumstance you are documenting, you can probably remember the day, time, and location that you heard the news. You sometimes might be able to even recollect the clothes you were wearing. These anecdotes are usually shared among friends and family but never written down. A news scrapbook is the ideal place to reminisce, and a wonderful keepsake for future generations to read. As grandchildren or great-grandchildren will flip through the album, they will get a firsthand account of the event from a beloved family member.

Not all newsworthy events are somber, and these albums are also wonderful areas to store memories that have a fun and exciting tone. Sports championship programs, or other means used to celebrate a news event, can be encapsulated in these albums as well. World Series game programs or newspaper headlines the day after a championship will add some areas of enjoyment and pleasure to these news scrapbooking albums.

Documenting sports victories

CHAPTER 20
Scrapbooking Gifts

Gifts that are related to scrapbooking provide both the satisfaction of furnishing a friend or family member with a sentimental present and the motivation to save memories. The most important thing to understand about scrapbooking gifts are the amount of time that will need to be dedicated to the projects and the cost involved.

Why a Gift Album?

It is easy to get caught up in the idea of scrapbooking particular subjects for a friend before you really think about the details of the project. A scrapbook takes a lot of energy and time, and often people begin these projects only to regret them halfway through. Gift albums do not need to have this kind of stress associated with them, and thinking about your reasoning behind the gift will help to determine if it is the right course of action.

Time and Money

Creating a gift album

Ask yourself why you are planning the gift. Does your friend or family member expect this from you, or is it something that you decided on your own? How much time do you have to devote to the project? After all, each scrapbook page will take at least one night, and depending on the length of your album, you may not realize the extent of the commitment you are making. When answering all of these questions, continue to think about alternatives to a scrapbook that will be just as thoughtful.

Figure the cost involved in creating an album of this nature. Standard scrapbooks plus all of the creative additions, coupled with the development of photography, will cost you a great deal of money. Sometimes people decide to create an album thinking that they will save money from purchasing a gift for a wedding or other special occasion. This usually results in the album costing more money than you would have spent on a standard gift.

Gift albums will sometimes reach to unexpected proportions, particularly because you will undoubtedly want to purchase materials that are best suited for the album and might cost a little more money than normal. After all, if you are giving away your handiwork, you want it to look its best!

FACTS

There are alternatives to creating standard scrapbooks as gifts. One style of album that you might not have thought about for your gift is a 5" × 7" album. This is not as popular as the larger styles but is still a worthy alternative. A small album will save you a great deal of money while maintaining the thought and care you put into it.

Plan of Action

A well thought-out plan is essential to creating a gift album. It should be taken seriously and given as much thought as if you were planning an event. Your budget, time, and the style of the album should all be determined in advance. Price the size of the actual album as well as related materials before you buy everything. You might find that the total cost is too high and you need to choose a smaller album to defray the expenses. The person receiving the gift will be just as happy with any size album you decide on using.

Additionally, plan ahead the time that you will need to create the album, particularly if you want to give the gift on a certain day. Be realistic in your goals and stick to the schedule to prevent any stress leading up to the deadline. For a larger 8.5" × 11" or 12" × 12" gift album, decide in advance how many pages the album will be and the titles for each page. This will help you to determine the length of time you need to create the final version.

Goals such as crafting one page per night or a few two-page spreads over a weekend are more practical than trying to complete the entire album in one week. Hopefully you have thought of this well enough in advance to meet these objectives.

A smaller album will take you less time, but do not be deceived by its size! The time it takes to design each page and think about your objectives will probably take just as long as larger albums, although the final creation of each page will usually result in a smaller amount of time per page.

ESSENTIALS

Find twelve of your favorite scrapbook layouts and take them to the local photocopy specialty store. Ask them to make high-quality color copies of these pages and then create a calendar for the coming year. These make wonderful holiday gifts for each member of the family, a group, or friends.

Whatever style of album you decide to use, one of the most essential elements is to create one theme that lasts throughout the book. This theme might consist of the same colors or patterns of paper, similar die-cuts, or the same kind of creative lettering. By using all of the same elements on each page, you will save time in the beginning stages of creating the album while maintaining consistency and movement as you turn each page. It is also sometimes less expensive to purchase a bulk amount of similar embell-ishments instead of separate decorations.

ABC . . . Easy As 1-2-3

Some of the best-constructed albums, along with wonderful gift options, are those that are considered "ABC" scrapbooks or "1-2-3" albums. These styles consist of each page following the alphabet or numbers with a theme related to the subject. ABC albums are popular among those in the scrap-booking circles, and they make a pleasant layout that people are frequently drawn to.

Brought to You by the Letter "B"

An ABC album is also a wonderful gift to give children. It acts as an educational tool while at the same time relating personal items about their lives. To create an alphabet album, decide on each theme or page title before you start the album.

If you are creating an education album for a child, decide on themes reflecting experiences that you can have together. As each topic occurs,

Example page from an ABC album

create the layout in the scrapbook together. Your result will be a book that teaches the alphabet with familiar experiences. Most likely your children will want to read the album often. These experiences should not be overwhelming or hard but things you can easily accomplish and then document.

For example, in an educational ABC album, you might start out with some basics such as "Apple Orchard" and document your visit to the local apple orchard. The book could continue with "Biking in the Park," "Cleaning the House," "Dancing to the Beat," and so on. The end result might be a trip to the zoo as a reward for completing the tasks and the album.

ABC albums are wonderful gifts for children, but a child may consider this a toy and destroy your hard work. Consider creating the album together and take it to the local copy center to be copied in color and spiral-bound. This new ABC book can then be given to your child as a new educational toy.

Let Me Count the Ways

A 1-2-3 album follows the same steps but might be a little easier to accomplish. For a teaching album, find your child's favorite objects and take pictures of them. Duplicate these with a color copier, and create the album by using them with the same numbers to which the layout corresponds.

If you would like to give a scrapbook gift to a travel companion to document a trip you recently took together, a 1-2-3 album would be a good way to keep the theme and layouts to a minimum. These can each be done on a two-page spread to ensure that the album contains all of the photos possible, but the format allows for a more generalized approach than the ABC album. An example of some titles and corresponding page materials include:

Scrapbook page from a 1-2-3 album

- One Trip to Ireland
- Two Friends Traveling
- Three U2 Sightings
- Four Speeding Tickets
- Five Youth Hostels
- Six Guinness Beers
- Seven Irish Towns
- Eight Pub Dinners
- Nine Historic Sites
- Ten Times to Return!

Giving Scrapbooking Basics

An alternative gift is to start somebody else on scrapbooking. You are probably always trying to get others interested in the craft anyway, so it is only natural for you to provide them with the materials to do so. This is a wonderful way to get others interested in your favorite pastime. When creating your gift, remember that to win a friend over in the craft of scrapbooking it is best to make the beginning as easy as possible.

Start Your Engines

Included in the gift should be the basics for beginners. Start them with an 8.5" × 11" album, one pair of straight-edged scissors, archival quality adhesives, a journaling pen, and patterned paper that will carry a theme throughout the book. It is a good idea to include some die-cuts and stickers that can help them to get started with the creative aspect of the layouts. Also provide letter-stickers or plastic alphabet templates for them. Asking them to produce their own creative lettering in the beginning might get too overwhelming. Most important, add notecards (or this *Everything*® book) that will explain to them the importance of using archival quality materials in the scrapbook page.

ESSENTIALS

When giving the gift of scrapbooking to someone, put all of the materials in one large basket that can then be used as a stepping stone for storing and organizing scrapbook materials.

An easy way to give somebody this type of gift is to encompass all of the materials into one theme. For example, if the receiver had once traveled to Disneyland but never documented her trip except to develop film, a scrapbook gift might include materials relating to this theme. You could provide an original Disney scrapbook, colorful embellishments, and characters that remind her of the vacation.

Throw in Some Extras

Scrapbooking coupon

One Free Evening of Scrapbooking!

Free Tools!
My Company!
No Kids!

Fine Print: You and I are going to spend an evening of fun together while we scrapbook. I will arrange a babysitter, and all you need to bring is your warm smile and your scrapbook materials. Food and drink provided. No purchase necessary. Void where prohibited.

To help your friend try out some elaborate scrapbooking tools, place in the gift some of your favorite gadgets on loan. You can include a note that explains how to use the materials and that she can keep them until she feels that she has mastered the techniques. This will allow her a little more excitement than simply using the basics, while not costing you as much money. It will also be another reason for you to get together to crop not long after the gift is provided.

Gift certificates can be found on most major scrapbooking sites. Slip one into a gift basket to allow the receiver to select the colors, stickers, die-cuts, and styles of papers she will use in her album. Another option is to add coupons to the gift that will give her the opportunity to request your assistance and companionship while creating the album. After all, there is no better way to scrapbook than with friends!

What Pictures?

The gift album you create does not have to follow the standard style you have come to know through scrapbooking. A wonderful present is to create an album that has all of the necessary items—stickers, embellishments, and layouts—everything but the photographs! Photo-less albums are most easily created with a 5" × 7" album that includes ten to fifteen pages. With a similar theme of mounting materials and well-placed embellishments throughout the book, creating this kind of album is quick and easy.

 **SSENTIALS**

A friend or family member who receives a photo-less gift album may not have acid-free adhesives to mount the pictures. Provide these adhesives for them with directions on their use, or better yet, give them a bag of photo corners to fasten each picture to the appropriate page.

Get Them Involved!

One style of photo-less album is an album created for a single purpose. For example, as a bridesmaid you might want to create a scrapbook that is devoted to the couple for their honeymoon. Use titles such as "Fly Away," "Lover's Crossing," "Romantic Evenings," and any other phrases more specifically related to their honeymoon location. Once they return from the trip, you can give them this album as a welcome-home gift and explain that they only need to add the pictures in the spaces that you provided. This is a simple way for them to be involved while at the same time making your life a lot easier.

Keep in mind that those who receive this style of gift album may not always have pictures that correspond to some specific titles you use! To ease this potential problem, use a plain card stock on top of patterned paper as photo-matting materials. This plain section will give them an area to journal if they do not have any photos that match. For example, a title "The Honeymoon Suite" would probably only be best if a photo was taken of the room or location. The area where the photo would have been placed is now an ideal spot for a written description of the surroundings.

Scrapbook page allowing the receiver to add the photos

A Scavenger Hunt

An alternative kind of gift album is one that includes a list of things to do in the page. It is similar to sending them on a scavenger hunt of items to recover, only for this they will need to obtain photos of each experience to place in the album you provided. For example, as an anniversary present to your husband, you might give him an album that has titles such as "Our First Date," "Popping the Question," and "Wedding Bliss." The two of you could then return to these memorable locations and take pictures of them for the album while at the same time traveling down memory lane.

FACTS

Gift albums make wonderful and thoughtful thank-you presents for parents, grandparents, teachers, professors, college roommates, counselors, bridesmaids, groomsmen, siblings, children, doctors, nurses, firefighters, police officers, husbands, coworkers, and so on.

Lending a Helping Hand

Gift albums have a greater meaning than simply the pleasure of giving a completed album to a friend or family member. It also can mean devoting your time to members of the community at large to assist in preserving historical records or volunteering within the community to create scrapbooks.

There are hundreds of opportunities to devote your time and energy into something meaningful and for the good of the community. Some of these include helping the local library catalogue historical and society documents, spending time at the local schools to ensure photos and important records are maintained in archival quality conditions, or volunteering in your church archives to help create displays that allow church members to view its history.

The Greatest Generation

One of the best kinds of scrap gifts that also benefits members of the community is to volunteer at a skilled nursing or long-term care facility. These centers are always looking for people who can bring a little creativity into the lives of elderly residents by using music and crafts. Additionally, a new face in the home is always a welcome change and an opportunity for the residents to tell stories about their childhood and family. Asking the elderly about their lives helps them to gain a sense of fulfillment and enjoyment, and devoting time to some residents who do not have family will be very meaningful.

There are often times when elderly residents of a skilled nursing facility no longer have any close family and friends, and consequently the key to preserving their heritage lies with them alone. Creating a scrapbook with these residents will be a project with many benefits. First and foremost, it will give the person something to look forward to every time you are scheduled to arrive. They will get excited about the project, and it will help to keep them busy while you are away by gathering photos or jotting down family notes during the week.

FACTS

Tombstone-rubbings are a popular trend to include in scrapbooks. To create them, tape a white paper to a tombstone and rub archival quality chalk against the impression of the stone. Ask permission of the cemetery, and ensure that the gravestone is in good condition before obtaining the rubbing. Use a chalk-spray once the rubbing is complete to maintain its quality.

Visiting Hours

Another way to volunteer and help is at the children's wing of your local hospital. Kids who need medical care over a long period of time can easily get bored with their surroundings, and as with a geriatric facility, a new face to keep them company has an immense impression on the quality of their lives.

Find a hospital that is willing to let you stay for a few hours at a time and think about the kinds of children you will want to spend your time helping. Those that are being treated for cancer or other long-term illnesses, as well as those recovering from lengthy operations, are wonderful targets for your volunteer project. However, any child who needs medical care, no matter how serious, will benefit from your willingness to help.

Both elderly residents and children who are recovering from illness will tire easily. Keep this in mind when you start to begin your scrapbooking project with these individuals. Start by teaching them the basics of the scrapbook page, and then let them create it at their own pace.

When visiting a long-term care facility, hospital wing, or other care center to work with individuals in scrapbooking, it will be difficult for you to choose which group to help. To alleviate this problem, ask the facility if you can teach a twenty-minute crash-course in scrapbooking to a gathering of residents. This should be a quick summary of the reasoning behind scrapbooking, emphatically expressing the benefit to each individual. Talk about the ability to honor in their scrapbooks those who help them every day and also document the ordeals that they are going through. Once they are recovered, a scrapbook will help them see how far they have come in this difficult time. When the class is over, they will let you know if they are interested in pursuing this craft with you.

CHAPTER 21

Scrapbooking as a Business

A s with any billion-dollar industry, the options for using scrapbooking as a business opportunity are endless and continually evolving. This chapter will discuss your choices for the business field of scrapbooking and give you some ideas on how to make money in this craft industry.

Direct Sales Consultants

When first thinking of turning scrapbooking into a business, many crafters automatically think of the direct-sales companies that helped to launch the industry in the late 1980s and early 1990s. After all, there have been many successful women who began their careers with one of these popular companies.

Selling Through Home Shows

A direct sales consultant for a major scrapbooking company will make most of her money by hosting home shows. These events bring potential buyers into a home where a beginning course in scrapbooking is taught. The difference between this kind of course and another is that all of the materials used and suggested for layouts will be the company product. As you move forward in your career, and as more and more of your friends become involved in scrapbooking, these home shows often turn into simple crops in which all gather in one location to scrapbook together.

When attending a home show, nobody is required to purchase any materials. In reality, however, joining a show and not purchasing any products is more easily said than done. According to the article "Scrapbooking—New Revenue Streams," on the Web site ✎*www.auntie.com*, most new customers at home shows spend $60–$100 on their first order. Additionally, those who frequent home shows will spend $30–$40 each subsequent time they attend. This is good news for a consultant, who might receive up to 30 percent of the profits depending on which direct sales company they represent.

Which Company Is Best?

When deciding on which direct-sales company to join as a consultant, consider both the short- and long-term benefits of each organization individually. They all provide excellent rationalization on why their organization is the best to work with, and for many it is hard to argue with their reasoning. Your needs and interests, however, should be the deciding factor on which company you decide to join.

Visit their homepages to read and compare the benefits. Since this project or career will take time to build, talk about the needs of each organization with your family just as you would before taking any kind of job. This is not something to rush into since many of the organizations require that you "buy into" the business.

To generalize, there are two basic styles of direct sales companies and organizations that you will come across in your research. The first includes a long-term approach by encouraging you to recruit others. Once you add consultants underneath you, it will catapult you to many higher levels of the career arrangement with a step approach to promotions. The more consultants you add, the higher you can climb. Additionally, the more recruits you add, the better the perks that you receive. These include earnings, bonuses, or merchandise. The second kind of company consultant is not multilevel. In this case, your profits come only from the merchandise you sell. You have less opportunity for residual income and perks, but in exchange you get greater flexibility in the time you devote to the organization.

As a consultant you will be able to earn several free products by selling a certain quota of materials. These can be used for your own personal scrapbooks or to give to friends or family members who host home shows. Additionally, you can use these free products to give as door prizes to entice more people to attend the event.

Most direct sales companies begin the process by asking you for a nominal fee. This cost is to cover supplies to get you started in your own consulting business. They include promotional materials, suggestions for proceeding, and supplies at a lower cost. You are also provided with a mentor who will be able to answer your questions and guide you though your first events.

These materials and instructions are essential to the success of beginning this business, but how you maintain it is almost entirely up to you. You have autonomy in how you promote your personal consulting skills and events. Many consultants even create their own Web sites that include printer-friendly how-to documents, event information, and details on how to order supplies.

Check the television listings when you host a consultant home-show! Popular television nights might prevent some people from attending. If you have the show on a weekend, use a Sunday afternoon instead of a Saturday. This will allow people who are traveling over the weekend to still attend if they return home early enough on Sunday.

To start the search for some choices in scrapbook consulting with a direct sales company, look at these Web sites for more information:

- *www.creativememories.com*
- *www.closetomyheart.com*
- *www.scrapinasnap.com*
- *www.stampinup.com*

Teaching the Craft

You might find that you are very good at instructing friends and family on the basics of scrapbooking and that many turn to you for help. If so, you might consider beginning to teach scrapbooking classes. Most local scrapbooking and chain craft stores offer classes. Additionally, many communities host adult classes through their park and recreation offices or community centers. They are always looking for teachers.

Getting Started

The basic way to make money teaching scrapbooking is to receive a portion of the student registration fee. This cost is usually based on the type of class and length of time. For example, a one-night "Scrapbooking 101" course might have a $10 registration fee, but a ten-week course devoted to the techniques of scrapbooking could cost $100.

Once you have secured the teaching post, find out if there are any rules governing selling products at these functions. You can secure wholesale products from company representatives and sell them to students for a small profit. Try not to raise the prices too much, however, because you want to be able to advertise your class to include inexpensive retail items.

QUESTIONS?

Can I make money by designing scrapbooks for others?
Yes! If you love the artistic elements of scrapbooking, consider starting a business where you actually create the scrapbooks or layout pages for customers! Charge by the size of the album, number of layouts, and cost of the materials.

Before you officially decide to teach, devise a class blueprint and try it out on friends and family. They will hopefully be honest with you about your means of presentation and offer suggestions for improvement. Setting up a mock class might also allow you to invite storeowners to see your teaching skills. Below is a sample lesson plan from a class devoted to scrapbooking quilt pages. Use this lesson plan for your class, or revise it to fit your individual taste and style.

Sample Lesson Plan

Class: Scrapbook Quilting
Level: Intermediate/Advanced Scrapbooking
Sessions: 2 evening sessions, 2–3 hours each
Cost: $20 per person, includes materials for one layout
Location: Community Center
Supplies required: blank scrapbook pages from an 8.5" × 11" and an 12" × 12" album, one journaling pen, and straight-edged scissors. Second session: patterned paper and pictures to design pages.
Summary:

1. The class begins with introductions. Students give their names, how long they have been scrapbooking, and why they want to create quilt pages.
2. Demonstrate the techniques and tools needed to create quilt pages.
3. Show samples of different styles of quilt pages. Have students learn the distinct names of popular quilt patterns.

4. Show how to create quilt images through shapes and stitching. Create one quilt page using the "Ohio Star" pattern.

5. Demonstrate the kinds of photos used for quilting and how to crop them into shapes usable for the layout page.

6. Create a quilt page using both a 8.5" × 11" and a 12" × 12" album. Have students assist in placement of materials.

7. Distribute materials and a quilt pattern to all students. Have them create the basics of the page using the materials provided.

8. (Class Two) Regroup and ask students to bring enough materials and photos for three quilt pages.

9. (Class Two) Distribute three patterns to the class and give basic instructions.

10. (Class Two) Have the class complete the three pages. Talk with each student to provide suggestions.

Writing for Riches

Many scrapbookers find that they are good writers who could probably do a fine job writing for any of the many scrapbooking magazines. The kinds of magazines that you can write for may be published in print or on the Internet. There are many wonderful publications devoted to the scrapbooking crowd, but be sure to look at other styles of magazines as well for your scrapbooking articles. This craft is branching out: magazines devoted to general crafts, women's audiences, and even business might be interested in your articles.

Most print magazines provide some opportunities to submit articles and pay a fee for articles that are published, but each publication will have different standards for accepting articles. If you are serious about publishing your writing, obtain a copy of the current year's *Writer's Market* at any local bookstore. This book is the Bible for freelance writers. It contains information on all magazines, providing details on the kinds of articles they accept, the required word count, contact information, the process for submitting articles, and payment rates.

Online magazines are another option. You many want to write articles for your own Web site, on which you intend to sell advertising space, for an already-established Web magazine, or for a retail scrapbooking Web site that is trying to lure shoppers to their Internet location. Contact these organizations by searching for the site administrator or office staff. Many Web sites will have a "Contact Us" or "Meet the Staff" section on their home page. Ask if they accept articles, and find out what steps they suggest you take toward getting published. Unlike printed magazines, the Internet path to writing materials for publication is not clearly defined. You may have to do some additional digging to locate the submission directions for each site.

Independent Scrapbooking Store

One of the most complicated yet rewarding scrapbooking businesses is a scrapbooking store. It takes a lot of hard work and a solid plan of action, but the end result could be a well-run personal business doing something that you love.

Create a Business Plan

The first step to opening a retail store is to create a business plan. This will help you to figure out how much money you will need up front, how to market to your target audience, and the details for inventory and space you will need. You will also probably need a loan if you do not have the capital to begin on your own.

A franchise is a company that lends out its trademarked name and system of doing business. Franchise operators pay a royalty fee to do business under the franchise name, and they return anywhere from 3 to 6 percent of monthly gross sales to the parent company.

It is probably best to purchase a couple of books about starting a business to teach you the basics. Local colleges might also offer classes on the subject and help you to write the business plan as an assignment. Once you feel you are ready, contact your local chamber of commerce or your state government's economic development center and ask if they have a mentoring program to help guide you along the way.

In your plan you might also consider franchising your store. This may seem too early to think about such a thing. However, some of the most successful franchises were not afterthoughts of a successful single business but instead were considered as options from the start. If you are thinking about franchising, it might impact the amount of square footage you buy or rent, the style of marketing that you use for the store, and the kinds of classes that you offer.

Research, Research, Research

When you are thinking about the store you would like to own, start to think about the details that you believe will make the store work. Do this by visiting other independent scrapbooking stores and get to know their store layout and methods of advertising. Talk with storeowners who are willing to give you some advice, particularly about things that they would do differently now that they have been involved in the industry for a few years. Be sure to let the storeowners know you are not in their immediate area to reassure them that you are not trying to steal their business.

ALERT

Many Web-based organizations claim to offer you a "free" credit report. The small print, however, shows that you are also purchasing their services for a thirty-day trial period and will be billed as soon as the thirty days is complete. Instead of going through this hassle, consider paying a small fee for this report which you will need for a business plan.

Store Décor

As you create your business plan, think about all of the details of the physical store. How do you want the store to feel when a customer walks in? These are things you need to consider from the get-go. You probably want customers to feel comfortable with a homey environment. This might mean a home-decorated feel with carpet and comfortable chairs to allow customers to sit and chat while they wait for friends to finish shopping.

The layout of the store will be a combination of personal taste and marketing sense. You will probably want to be sure to have a plethora of samples posted throughout the store, on the walls, and in scrapbooks displayed on stands that are high enough for customers to flip though. Use the materials you are trying to sell for these displays, and feature different styles on different days. Additionally, talk with material supply companies like Susan Branch and Mrs. Grossman's who can set up kiosk-like displays that adds a wonderful visual element to the store.

FACTS

Andrea Grossman founded Mrs. Grossman's Paper Company in 1975. Her company now has over 100 employees and 300 new designs of stickers that are printed twenty-four hours a day, as well as other product lines such as cards, backs, and craft kits. You can arrange to tour the plant by contacting the Consumer Relations Department at 800/429-4549. Visit *www.mrsgrossmans.com* for more information.

The window displays will be most important. As standard as this craft has become, there are still many people who do not understand its significance in safely archiving family memories. Additionally, some people who do know about the popularity of the craft are continually brushing it off as a pop fad. Your goal for window displays is to bring people who walk by and admire the samples and displays into the store. It will hopefully pique their curiosity enough to get them interested in looking into some scrapbooking choices. Once you get them into the store, the rest is up to you!

Starting a Retail Web Site

The success of retail Web sites also depends on some of the same necessities as a physical retail store. A business plan is needed as well as a significant sum of money to get you started. You would be wise to speak with other retail Web owners to ask for tips on starting your own site. The difference in this research is that you may want to do your inquiries with retail sites that offer arts and crafts products other than scrapbooking. Unlike physical stores whose location prevents you from targeting the same customers, Internet retail stores all share the same target audience. Your potential competitors may not be that willing to lend you a helping hand.

ESSENTIALS

Learn how to create a Web site! Learning code such as HTML will save you some money on the upkeep of your Web site, and while you will eventually need to have someone help to maintain it, defraying these high costs with some expertise of you own will keep you one step ahead of the game.

Some initial costs are Web development and the creation of a secure system for credit card purchases. You might think that the overhead costs of a Web site are much less because you do not owe rent or a mortgage. The truth is that it costs a great deal of money to create and maintain a Web site. Scrapbooking supply sites that offer photos of products sometimes have an even greater technology overhead because of all the intricate details in the materials. There may be hundreds of styles of patterned papers and stickers, and showing them all is important.

FACTS

The Service Corps of Retired Executives (SCORE) has over 11,000 volunteers providing counseling to America's small businesses. They are "dedicated to aiding in the formation, growth, and success of small businesses nationwide." Visit their Web site for information about counseling, e-mail counseling, client success stories, business resources, and volunteer opportunities at *www.score.org*.

Many retail outlets on the Web will provide their own versions of a scrapbooking newsletter and layout tips. This will get crafters to your site during Web searches for the subjects listed. Advertising for an online retail site will also capture a different audience—one that is connected and comfortable with the Internet.

The day that you launch the Web site you will probably want to market the site in advertising space on scrapbooking message board sites, online scrapbooking magazines, and other places that you have researched and found scrapbookers to frequent. Additionally, you may be interested in letting some scrapbookers who frequent message boards know about the site launch and about your Web promotions.

Scrapbooking Newsletters

Publishing your own scrapbooking newsletter will be one of the easiest ways to make an income in the scrapbooking field. It may not start out as a lot of money, but if you have some patience it will usually result in some small profit. The best advantage to creating a scrapbooking newsletter is the minimal cost involved in launching the project. Newsletters are easy and fun, and they can get you in touch with a great number of people. Depending on your personal style and interests, the newsletter can focus on tips, new scrapbooking methods, unique materials, news of new online sites, or a combination. There are two styles of scrapbooking newsletters: the customary paper newsletter, and the more technology-oriented Web newsletter.

The Paper Chase

With all of the increases in technology, there is something very comforting about an old-fashioned paper newsletter. It is much easier on the eyes and allows the information to be handy at all times. Paper newsletters will probably not make you that much money at first, but once you develop a large enough support base, you can make some money from the subscriptions themselves. Eventually, you will be able to tell advertisers how many people read your newsletter. Selling advertising space can bring in some big bucks.

Web Newsletters

The increased popularity of the Internet has really refocused how many people provide information to particular groups. Scrapbooking on the Internet has immense popularity, and someone who is invested in the craft will often search long and hard for new information. The big difference is that your monetary gain from this newsletter will now come from advertisers instead of subscribers. You can also have paying subscribers, but with the amount of free information on the Internet they are harder to secure.

ESSENTIALS

You do not need a direct sales company to host a crop! Organize the location for the crop, provide materials donated from scrapbooking supply stores, refreshments, and ask everyone to bring one tool for sharing. By charging a small fee for your efforts (about $5 per person), you might be able to make $50–$100 in a night.

Consider owning your own domain name for this newsletter. Many people start by using a service that offers free Web site hosting as long as they can advertise on your site. This system has its problems because the amount of space for information is limited, and as such it limits the length of your newsletter. Additionally, Web newsletters make their money from the advertising, and beginnings at this kind of site will in some cases prevent you from doing the same.

Appendix A

Scrapbooking Web Links

Scrapbooking Message Boards

- Babycenter Scrapbooking Board:
  www.babycenter.com/bbs/11984/

- Collected Memories:
  www.collectedmemories.com/Ideas/MessageBoard.html

- Cropping Queens:
  www.croppingqueens.com
  www.board/index.htm

- Parentsplace Message Board:
  http://boards.parentsplace.com/cgi-bin/boards/scrapbooks

- Two Too Cool
  Scrapbooking Board:
  www.22cool.com/bbs1/

Scrapbooking Retreats

- Crazed Croppers
  Weekend Getaways:
  www.crazedcroppers.com

- Crop-A-Lot
  Scrapbooking Retreats:
  www.cropalot.com

- Dream Events, Inc.:
  www.dreameventsinc.com

- Gotta Crop Ultimate Scrappers
  Getaway: *www.gottacrop.com*

- Memories for Scrappers
  and Stampers:
  www.memoriesexpo.com

- Scrap and Spa:
  www.scrapandspa.com

- Scrapaway:
  www.scrapaway.com

- Scrapbook Camp:
  www.scrapbookcamp.com

- Scrapper's Roundup:
  www.scrappersroundup.com

Web Magazines and Resources

- About Scrapbooking:
  http://scrapbooking.about.com

- Aspiring to Greatness Poems,
  Quotes and Stories:
  www.aspiring-community.com

- Association of Crafts and
  Creative Industries:
  www.accicrafts.org

- Crazy For Scrappin':
  www.alysta.com/scrapbooking

- Creative Scrapbooking:
  www.creativescrapbooking.com

- Cropping Queens:
  www.croppingqueens.com

- Family Tree Magazine:
  www.familytreemagazine.com

- Font Garden:
  www.fontgarden.com

- Graceful Bee:
  www.gracefulbee.com

- Hobby Industry Association:
  www.hobby.org

- Lots of Layouts:
  www.lolsb.com

- One Scrappy Site:
  www.geocities.com/onescrappysite

- Scrap Easy On-Line Magazine:
  www.scrapeasy.com

- Scrap Network.com:
  www.scrapnetwork.com

- Scrapbook Addict
  Product Review:
  www.scrapbookaddict.com

- Scrapbooking.com:
  http://scrapbooking.com

- ScrapLink.com:
  www.scraplink.com

- Scrappin' By Alaine:
  www.scrappingbyalaine.com

- ScrappyDeesigns:
  www.scrappydeesigns.com

Genealogy Sites

- Cyndi's List:
  www.cyndislist.com

- Family Search:
  www.familysearch.org

- Genealogy.com:
  www.genealogy.com

- National Archives
  Record Administration:
  www.nara.gov

- National Genealogical Society:
  www.ngsgenealogy.org

- The Library of Congress:
  http://lcweb.loc.gov

U.S. Census Bureau:
www.census.gov

Web Retail and Supply Stores

Absolutely Everything:
www.absolutelyeverything.com/ suppl.htm

Accu-Cut:
www.accucut.com

Addicted 2 Scrapbooks:
www.addicted2scrapbooks.com

AlphaPics:
http://alphapics.safeshopper.com

Alpine Import Craft Supplies:
www.alpineimport.com

American Scrapbook:
www.americanscrapbook.com

Annie's Scrapbooks:
http://capitolway.com/annies

AnnKorp Rubber Stamping & Scrapbooking Supplies:
www.annkorp.com

Archival Products:
www.archival.com/ text/binder.html

Basic Bear Designs:
www.basicbear.com

Bits and Pieces:
www.scrapbooksupply.com

Blooming Ideas:
http://bloomingideas. safeshopper.com

Border Maker:
www.bordermaker.com

Buttonmart:
http://buttonmart.freeyellow.com/in dex.html

Calico Skies:
www.calico-skies.com/scrap.htm

Canadian Scrapper:
http://canadianscrapper. safeshopper.com

Caren's Crafts:
http://scrapbooking4fun.com

Carolee's Creations:
http://caroleescreations.com

CatScrapFever Web Designs:
www.catscrapfever.com

Christie's Creations:
www.christiescreations.com

Classic Creations by Shawn:
www.thevine.net/classic/ index.htm

Claudia's Clipart:
www.claudiasclipart.com

Collected Memories:
www.collectedmemories.com

Color Spots:
www.colorspots.com

Computer Scrapbooking:
www.computerscrapbooking.com

Crafter's Toybox:
www.crafterstoybox.com

Crafty Creations:
www.crafty1.com

Creative Borders:
www.creativeborders.com

Creative Shop.com:
www.creativityshop.com/ scrapbook

Creative Xpress:
http://creativexpress.com

Crop Paper Scissors:
www.croppaperscissors.com

Crop-In-Style:
www.cropinstyle.com

Cropoholics:
www.cropaholics.com

Cropper Hopper:
www.cropperhopper.com

C-thru Ruler:
www.cthruruler.com

Cute Stuff Inside:
www.cutestuffinside.com

Cut-N-Fun:
www.cutnfun.com

Dalee Book Company:
www.daleebook.com

Darlene's Scrapbooking:
www.dscrapbooking.com

Dayco:
www.daycodiecuts.com

Debby's Things:
www.debbysthings.com

Designer Stencils:
www.designerstencils.com

Die Cuts with a View:
www.diecutswithaview.com

- Dmarie:
  www.dmarie.com

- Down Home Designs:
  *www.hydrotoys.com/
  downhomedesigns*

- Elm Tree Creations
  Journaling Companion:
  www.elmtreecreations.com

- Emagination Crafts, Inc.:
  www.emaginationcrafts.com

- Enterprising Designs:
  www.enterprisingdesigns.com

- Everything Scrapbooks:
  www.everythingscrapbooks.com

- EZScrap.net:
  www.ezscrap.net

- Family Preserves:
  www.scrapbookcanada.com

- Fiskars:
  www.fiskars.com

- Frame-Ups by My Mind's Eye,
  Inc.: *www.frame-ups.com*

- Frances Meyer, Inc.:
  www.francesmeyer.com

- Gateway Memories:
  www.gatewaymemories.com

- Generations by Hazel:
  www.generationsbyhazel.com

- Gone Scrappin':
  www.gonescrappin.com

- Grammy's Scrapbook House:
  *http://grammyscrapbookhouse.
  safeshopper.com*

- Hand Cart Heritage Albums:
  *http://handcartheritage.
  safeshopper.com*

- Heirlooms from the Heart:
  *http://heirloomsfromtheheart.
  safeshopper.com*

- Hobby Lobby:
  www.hobbylobby.com

- HollyCraft:
  www.hollycraft.com

- Home & Crafts:
  www.homeandcrafts.com

- Hot off the Press:
  www.hotp.com

- I Love Stickers:
  www.ilovestickers.com

- Jenny Craft:
  www.jennycraft.com

- Karen's Scrappin' Kupboard:
  www.karensscrappin.com.au

- Keeping Memories Alive:
  www.scrapbooks.com

- Kingly Kreations:
  www.kinglykreations.com

- Luv 2 Scrapbook:
  www.luv2scrapbook.com

- Make It a Memory:
  www.makeitamemory.net

- Making Memories Last:
  www.makingmemorieslast.com

- Memories and Milestones:
  *www.memoriesand
  milestones.com*

- Memories:
  www.memories.com

- Michaels: The Arts and Crafts
  Store: *www.michaels.com*

- Missy Made It:
  www.missymadeit.com

- More-Than-Memories.com:
  www.more-than-memories.com

- Mrs. Grossman's Stickers:
  www.mrsgrossmans.com

- My Scrapbook Stuff:
  www.myscrapbookstuff.com

- My Sister's Scrapbook:
  www.mysistersscrapbook.com

- My-Memories:
  *http://my-memories.
  safeshopper.com*

- Narda's Good Stuff:
  www.nardasgoodstuff.com

- NRN Designs:
  www.nrndesigns.com

- O' Scrap!:
  www.imaginations-inc.com

- Paper Addict:
  www.paperaddict.com

- Paper Adventures:
  www.paperadventures.com

- Paper Piecing Patch:
  www.paperpiecingpatch.com

- Patchwork Memories:
  www.patchworkmemories.com

- Pebbles in My Pocket:
  www.pebblesinmypocket.com

Perfect Scraps:
http://perfectscraps.com

Pieces of You:
www.piecesofu.com

Preservation Scrapbook Co.:
www.preservations-scrapsite.com

Provocraft:
www.provocraft.com

Remember It Well:
www.rememberitwell.com

Remember When On Line:
www.rememberwhenonline.com

Scrap N' Stuff:
www.scrapnstuff.com

Scrap that Smile:
www.scrapthatsmile.com

Scrapadoodledoo:
www.scrapadoodledoo.com

Scrapbook 101:
www.scrapbook101.com

Scrapbook Bargain:
www.scrapbookbargain.com

Scrapbook Barn:
www.scrapbookbarn.com

Scrapbook Basics:
www.scrapbookbasics.com

Scrapbook Borders:
www.scrapbookborders.com

Scrapbook Central:
www.scrapbookcentral.com

Scrapbook SuperStore:
*www.bestoftimes.com/
catalog.htm*

Scrapbook Utopia:
www.scrapbookutopia.com

Scrapbook-Creations:
http://scrapbook-creations.com

Scrapoholic's Anonymous, Inc.:
www.scrapaholics.com

Scrap-oodles:
www.scrapoodles.com

Scrappapers.net:
www.scrappapers.net

Scrapper's Haven:
www.scrappershaven.com

Scrappin' at the Scrap Patch:
www.scrappatch.com

Scrappin' Basics:
www.scrappinbasics.com

Scrappin' Fools:
www.scrappinfools.com

Scrappin' Happy:
www.scrappinhappy.com

Scrappin' Safari:
www.scrapnsafari.com

Scrapping Creations:
www.scrappingcreations.com

Scrapping Time:
www.scrappingtime.com

Scrapramento:
www.scrapramento.com

Scraps to Treasures:
www.scrapstotreasures.com

Scraptastic:
www.shopatscraptastic.com

Simply Creative:
*http://simplycreativecrafts.
safeshopper.com*

Simply Stickers:
www.simplystickers.com

Southern Splash Scrapbook
Supplies:
www.southernsplash.com

Stampin' and Scrappin':
www.stampinscrappin.com

Sticker Bar:
www.stickerbar.com

Sticker Planet:
www.stickerplanet.com

Sticker Store and More:
www.stickerstoreandmore.com

Stickers Galore:
www.stickersgalore.com

Stickopotamus:
www.stickopotamus.com

StickerIt.com:
www.stickerit.com

Still Making Memories:
www.stillmakinmemories.com

Stop-N-Crop:
www.stopncrop.com

Strawberries and Dreams:
www.strawberriesanddreams.com

Super Scrapbook Supplies:
www.superscrapbooksupplies.com

Tapestry in Time:
www.tapestryintime.com

- The Attic:
  www.atticalbums.com

- The Crop Café:
  www.cropcafe.com

- The Cropping Shoppe:
  www.croppingshoppe.com

- The Fox Den:
  www.foxtales.net

- The Heartland Paper Company:
  www.heartlandpaper.com

- The Internet Boutique:
  www.iboutique.com

- The Kreative Korner:
  www.thekreativekorner.com

- The Page Planner:
  www.thepageplanner.com

- The Paper Attic:
  www.thepaperattic.com

- The Photo Safe:
  www.thephotosafe.com

- The Preservation Station:
  www.preservationstation.com

- The Printer's Daughter:
  www.theprintersdaughter.com

- The Punch Palace:
  www.punchpalace.com

- The Robin's Nest:
  www.robinsnest-scrapbook.com

- The Scrapbook Nook:
  www.scrapbook-nook.com

- The Sticker Stop:
  www.stickerstop.com

- The Uptown Design Company:
  www.uptowndesign.com

- Three Sisters Antiques and
  Collectibles: *www.3sis.com*

- Times to Cherish by Current:
  www.timestocherish.com

- TLCScraps:
  www.tlcscraps.com

- Tomorrow's Memories:
  www.tomemories.com

- Two Peas in a Bucket:
  www.twopeasinabucket.com

- Victoria's Keepsakes:
  www.victoriaskeepsakes.com

- What Memories Are Made Of:
  www.memoriesinthemaking.com

- You're Invited:
  www.scrapbookingwithus.com

APPENDIX B

Magazine Subscription and Submission Information

Creating Keepsakes Magazine
Subscriber Services
P.O. Box 469007
Escondido, CA 92046-9007
Phone: 888/247-5282
International: 760/745-2809
Fax: 760/745-7200
www.creatingkeepsakes.com

Editorial Submissions
Creating Keepsakes
354 Mountain Way Drive Abb
Orem, UT 84058-5122

Electronic Submissions: Send the email to
editorial@creatingkeepsakes.com. Include your scan
as an attachment to the message. *Note:* Attached
files must be less than 500K. If your layout is
accepted, you will be asked to mail a copy of the
original.

Ivy Cottage Scrapbooking Magazine
Subscriber Services
P.O. Box 50688
Provo, UT 84605
Phone: 888/303-1375
Fax: 801/235-8091
E-mail: *info@ivycottagecreations.com*
www.ivycottagecreations.com

Submissions
Cottage Creations
P.O. Box 50688
Provo, UT 84605-0588

Electronic Submissions: E-mail scanned submissions to
submissions@ivycottagecreations.com. Write your
name, phone number, address, and e-mail (if
available) on each page submission. The page must
be an original idea—no copied ideas will be accepted.
Write detailed instructions on how you constructed
each page. List the brand name, color, etc. of all
products used, including paper, scissors, templates,
pens, stamps, ink color, software, fonts, etc.

Memory Makers Magazine
12365 Huron Street, Suite 500
Denver, CO 80234-3438
Phone: 303/920-5356
Fax: 303/452-3582
www.memorymakersmagazine.com

Submissions
Memory Makers
Idea Coordinator
12365 Huron Street, Suite 500
Denver, CO 80234-3438

PaperKuts Scrapbook Magazine
P.O. Box 91836
Long Beach, CA 90809-9960
Phone: 888/881-5861
www.paperkuts.com
E-mail: *subscriptions@paperkuts.com*

Editorial Submissions
PaperKuts
232 West 540 North Holland Square
Orem, UT 84057
E-mail: *layouts@paperkuts.com* or
articles@paperkuts.com

The Rubber Stamper
Customer Service
P.O. Box 420
Manalapan, NJ 07726
Phone: 800/969-7176 or 732/446-4900 ext. 510
www.rubberstamper.com

Design Submissions
The Rubber Stamper
225 Gordons Corner Road
Box 420
Manalapan, NJ 07726

Please make sure all projects are clearly labeled
with your name, phone number, and stamp credits.
If you would like your submission returned, please
include a self-addressed stamped envelope.

Index

THE EVERYTHING CANDLEMAKING BOOK

By M. J. Abadie

With candles, you can set a mood, lift spirits, or a bring a sense of celebration to any occasion. Home candlemaking is not only much more economical than buying premade candles-it's also a lot more fun! Easy-to-follow stops lead you through the process of candlemaking-from making simple tapers and columns to candles that are layered, molded, appliquéd, scented, or twisted. Beautiful full-color photographs provide inspiration for creativity, whether you're designing your own unique shapes and color combinations, or attempting advanced techniques.

Trade paperback, $12.95
1-58062-623-8, 304 pages

OTHER *EVERYTHING*® BOOKS BY ADAMS MEDIA CORPORATION

Everything® **Pregnancy Organizer**
$15.00, 1-58062-336-0

Everything® **Project Management Book**
$12.95, 1-58062-583-5

Everything® **Puppy Book**
$12.95, 1-58062-576-2

Everything® **Quick Meals Cookbook**
$14.95, 1-58062-488-X

Everything® **Resume Book**
$12.95, 1-58062-311-5

Everything® **Romance Book**
$12.95, 1-58062-566-5

Everything® **Running Book**
$12.95, 1-58062-618-1

Everything® **Sailing Book, 2nd Ed.**
$12.95, 1-58062-671-8

Everything® **Saints Book**
$12.95, 1-58062-534-7

Everything® **Scrapbooking Book**
$14.95, 1-58062-729-3

Everything® **Selling Book**
$12.95, 1-58062-319-0

Everything® **Shakespeare Book**
$14.95, 1-58062-591-6

Everything® **Slow Cooker Cookbook**
$14.95, 1-58062-667-X

Everything® **Soup Cookbook**
$14.95, 1-58062-556-8

Everything® **Spells and Charms Book**
$12.95, 1-58062-532-0

Everything® **Start Your Own Business Book**
$12.95, 1-58062-650-5

Everything® **Stress Management Book**
$14.95, 1-58062-578-9

Everything® **Study Book**
$12.95, 1-55850-615-2

Everything® **T'ai Chi and QiGong Book**
$12.95, 1-58062-646-7

Everything® **Tall Tales, Legends, and Other Outrageous Lies Book**
$12.95, 1-58062-514-2

Everything® **Tarot Book**
$12.95, 1-58062-191-0

Everything® **Thai Cookbook**
$14.95, 1-58062-733-1

Everything® **Time Management Book**
$12.95, 1-58062-492-8

Everything® **Toasts Book**
$12.95, 1-58062-189-9

Everything® **Toddler Book**
$14.95, 1-58062-592-4

Everything® **Total Fitness Book**
$12.95, 1-58062-318-2

Everything® **Trivia Book**
$12.95, 1-58062-143-0

Everything® **Tropical Fish Book**
$12.95, 1-58062-343-3

Everything® **Vegetarian Cookbook**
$12.95, 1-58062-640-8

Everything® **Vitamins, Minerals, and Nutritional Supplements Book**
$12.95, 1-58062-496-0

Everything® **Weather Book**
$14.95, 1-58062-668-8

Everything® **Wedding Book, 2nd Ed.**
$14.95, 1-58062-190-2

Everything® **Wedding Checklist**
$7.95, 1-58062-456-1

Everything® **Wedding Etiquette Book**
$7.95, 1-58062-454-5

Everything® **Wedding Organizer**
$15.00, 1-55850-828-7

Everything® **Wedding Shower Book**
$7.95, 1-58062-188-0

Everything® **Wedding Vows Book**
$7.95, 1-58062-455-3

Everything® **Weddings on a Budget Book**
$9.95, 1-58062-782-X

Everything® **Weight Training Book**
$12.95, 1-58062-593-2

Everything® **Wicca and Witchcraft Book**
$14.95, 1-58062-725-0

Everything® **Wine Book**
$12.95, 1-55850-808-2

Everything® **World War II Book**
$12.95, 1-58062-572-X

Everything® **World's Religions Book**
$12.95, 1-58062-648-3

Everything® **Yoga Book**
$12.95, 1-58062-594-0

*Prices subject to change without notice.

EVERYTHING KIDS' SERIES!

Everything® **Kids' Baseball Book, 2nd Ed.**
$6.95, 1-58062-688-2

Everything® **Kids' Cookbook**
$6.95, 1-58062-658-0

Everything® **Kids' Joke Book**
$6.95, 1-58062-686-6

Everything® **Kids' Mazes Book**
$6.95, 1-58062-558-4

Everything® **Kids' Money Book**
$6.95, 1-58062-685-8

Everything® **Kids' Monsters Book**
$6.95, 1-58062-657-2

Everything® **Kids' Nature Book**
$6.95, 1-58062-684-X

Everything® **Kids' Puzzle Book**
$6.95, 1-58062-687-4

Everything® **Kids' Science Experiments Book**
$6.95, 1-58062-557-6

Everything® **Kids' Soccer Book**
$6.95, 1-58062-642-4

Everything® **Travel Activity Book**
$6.95, 1-58062-641-6

Available wherever books are sold!
To order, call 800-872-5627, or visit us at everything.com

Everything® is a registered trademark of Adams Media Corporation.